*The American
Immigration Collection*

Intelligence and Immigration

CLIFFORD KIRKPATRICK

Arno Press and *The New York Times*

NEW YORK 1970

Reprint Edition 1970 by Arno Press Inc.

Reprinted from a copy in
The Kansas State University Library

LC# 76-129405
ISBN 0-405-00558-X

The American Immigration Collection—Series II
ISBN for complete set 0-405-00543-1

Manufactured in the United States of America

INTELLIGENCE AND IMMIGRATION

MENTAL MEASUREMENT MONOGRAPHS

SERIAL NO. 2

INTELLIGENCE
AND
IMMIGRATION

BY

CLIFFORD KIRKPATRICK, PH.D.

BALTIMORE

THE WILLIAMS & WILKINS COMPANY

1926

Composed and Printed at the
WAVERLY PRESS
for
The Williams & Wilkins Company
Baltimore, Md., U. S. A.

CONTENTS

CHAPTER IV

CHAPTER V

TO MY PARENTS

CONTENTS

INTRODUCTION

The objectives of this investigation may first be stated in general and then in more specific form. In general the purpose is to investigate the effect of past immigration, as made up of different nationality groups upon the mental capacity of the present American population and to consider the implication of the findings for a scientific immigration policy. More specifically the aims are: (1) to consider the significance and nature of intelligence, (2) to bring together the data bearing on the relative intelligence of different immigrant stocks in this country, (3) to present a detailed study of certain immigrant groups investigating (a) relative mental levels and (b) the influence of the language factor on the mental test scores, (4) to discuss the implication of the findings for our immigration policy and to make suggestions for the future.

It is clearly recognized that it is very difficult to maintain a purely detached, objective and scientific attitude in any matter where comparisons of groups or races are involved, as shown by the character of a considerable proportion of the literature in this field. It is attempted, however, to maintain a cautious and critical spirit by an appreciation of the difficulties both subjective and objective. Comparisons of groups while necessary for an evaluation of the effect of immigration are very likely to be invidious and are perhaps only justified by the principle that in the long run, carefully determined scientific truth brings a preponderance of good over evil results.

ACKNOWLEDGMENTS

The writer is under a great obligation to a large number of Superintendents, Principals, Priests and teachers, whom it is impossible to mention singly, but whose generous cooperation and assistance made the research possible. The writer is also indebted to the late Professor Edmund Sanford of Clark University for aid in obtaining financial assistance from that institution, to Professor Carl Kelsey who very kindly undertook the wearisome task of reading the manuscript, and above all to Professor Kimball Young who has given advice and encouragement, and whose pioneer work in the field has been most helpful.

CHAPTER I

The immigration problem is indeed perplexing but it is not a new one in the history of the world nor one that presents features here in America differing from the fundamental pattern. Men live in groups and are more or less perfectly adjusted to their physical environment, tilling the soil and utilizing the natural resources. Through interaction with environment and with each other culture comes into being, in material forms such as machines and buildings, and in immaterial forms comprising customs, tradition, institutions, tastes, values, standards of living, forms of government and the like. Now when men of a certain group become maladjusted to their physical environment because of pressure of population on resources or because of exclusion from the bounty of nature by a dominating class, or more rarely, if they become maladjusted to their culture because of political or religious heterodoxy, they tend to migrate. The emigration of course depends on means of transportation and communication. There must be a stimulus of what seems to be a more favorable environment and the possibility of response through adequate transportation facilities.

The problem of immigration then, is the problem of adjustment of a new group of individuals set in motion by these causes to an old group of a given biological type adjusted to a given environment and possessing a given culture or civilization. The effect of the movement on the established group will depend first on the numbers of the new comers, second on their characteristics acquired from their previous physical and cultural environment, and thirdly upon the innate characteristics of the new comers, physical and mental.

The number of immigrants and their cultural traits, such as standard of living, degree of skill, literacy, political ideals, etc. are the basis of the immigration problem in its economic aspects.

1

and viewed as a matter of assimilation. These considerations are important, and that of numbers is rendered more so by investigations of Thompson, East and other Malthusians who show that the land resources of even the United States are decidedly limited and that at the present rate of increase, saturation is a matter of decades rather than of centuries. This discussion, however, will be limited to a single innate trait, that of mental capacity or intelligence.

Considering intelligence in a broad sense as innate ability it is apparent that its importance depends on which of two opposing views is accepted. There are three factors underlying social phenomenon, the physical environment, inherited characteristics, and culture. The conflict of opinion arises from extreme views held on either side as to the relative importance of the last two factors. Both the hereditarians and environmentalists defend their causes with almost religious fervor. On the one hand we have sociologists such as Ward together with the cultural anthropologists, and on the other Galton and Pearson together with such extremists as Grant and Stoddard. Among the psychologists and educators we have Terman (124) on the one side with Bagley leading the forces of opposition. As a broad proposition, the question is not worth discussion for nature never exists apart from nurture. The matter resolves itself into a practical question as to which of the two variables can best be controlled to obtain a specific desired end.

There is no denying the importance of problems of assimilation or the success that may follow attempts to improve the immigrant by education and cultural contact, but the innate qualities of the new comers deserve more consideration than they yet have received. High grade germplasm often leads to better results than a high per capita school expenditure. Definite limits are set by heredity, and immigrants of low innate ability cannot by any amount of Americanization be made into intelligent American citizens capable of appropriating and advancing a complex culture. A decline in the innate capacities of a people is a slow process that cannot be readily detected but if degeneration ever sets in, a rigid selection is necessary before a higher level of innate abilities is restored.

INTELLIGENCE AND SOCIAL PROGRESS

For the cultural determinist and those inclined to that point of view cultural change corresponds to social change. Culture floats over and above the static and unchanging factor of the human organism and carries the seeds of its own independent development. Antecedents combine and recombine in such a fashion that the rate of growth is a function of that which has gone before, the process being almost such as to be represented in a rough fashion by a logarithmic curve. Ogburn (87, 73–142) has argued effectively for this point of view and there is no denying the large element of truth in the doctrine. Nevertheless, it must be remembered that a constant interaction between the organic or biological factor and the cultural is necessary. The existing culture must be absorbed into a human mind before a new combination or invention is possible. This means that when the volume of culture increases tremendously as it has done in recent years greater and greater mental power is required to absorb and recombine the cultural elements, and the greater the number of such individuals the greater the speed with which the recombination of the cultural elements into a new invention will take place.

Even if this need were admitted, it might be argued that only a few superior leaders are necessary and that in this age of machinery intelligence is only a handicap to the modern helot who is tending to become a mere part of the machine he tends. This undesirable state of affairs, however, is not likely to occur, for increased use of automatic machinery will create a demand for skilled repairmen rather than mere machine tenders. On other grounds it is unlikely that a concentration of intelligence in a few superior individuals would alone be sufficient to make for progress either material, social or intellectual. Civilization tends to advance on the two legs of invention and imitation. Intelligence is required to appreciate intelligence and history is already replete with examples of men in advance of their time or men surrounded by clods incapable of discriminative imitation.

INTELLIGENCE AND DEMOCRACY

Another phase of the matter is the fact that complexity of culture especially in the forms of social organization and economic interdependence have developed hand in hand with democracy. The "Great Society," for better or worse, is organized on a democratic basis and thus the destinies of a civilization infinitely complex is in the hands of the many. It can be readily shown that the world is now bound together so that events in one place may be of infinite importance to men half a world away. Masses of people determine peace or war and participation or non-participation in world affairs, whose vital significance and implication they are likely not to appreciate. Perhaps the mass of people are manipulated by propaganda so that leaders really determine the policies, yet the best propaganda is not the best statesmanship and immunity to propaganda depends on intelligence. Since the leaders are chosen, the quality of the leadership depends on the intelligence of the many, and also its objectives, for most policies are framed with an eye to popular prejudice and an ear cocked to hear the murmurings of the vox populi. The dependence on public opinion gives rise to many examples of what Lippman would call, "The cult of the second best." In England there was a popular pressure for a short sighted and impossible peace treaty which was forced upon the world against the better judgment of the leaders. Like wise in the United States, in internal economic policy, and in the matter of foreign debts, leaders are forced to give their second best in leadership.

Democracy in the sense of control by public opinion depends on education and enlightenment and if it is shown that education depends on native intelligence, then this must be taken into account.

Is not intelligence required for critical selection of the sound leadership which is so necessary in a complex world where false steps may spell disaster. It is true as Wells and others have pointed out that we are engaged in a race between education and catastrophe but education pre-supposes intelligence and hence the need of a eugenic policy which shall include a more scientific control of immigration.

THE NATURE OF INTELLIGENCE

The term intelligence or mental capacity has been used in a broad and general way but before concrete investigations can be presented, the terms used and the assumptions made must be given a brief analysis. The meaning of intelligence must be made clear, it must be shown to be hereditary, and it must be shown to be measurable or at least subject to estimate, in order that comparisons of the intelligence of various nativity groups may have real significance.

If the nature of intelligence be considered from the viewpoint of genetic psychology, it is evident that man is more intelligent than the lower animals in that his larger brain makes possible the formation of associations which store up past experience and increase adaptability to new situations. By means of memory man binds time and space and the projection of past experience into the future makes possible foresight and control (89, 265). The appropriation and advancement of culture is simply the acquirement of experience, either personally, or from others in the group, and its utilization to meet new situations. This process is made possible by virtue of innate capacity for learning, or in other words by intelligence.

While there are many shades of opinion among psychologists as to the nature of intelligence (121), some like Colvin and Buckingham cut the Gordian knot by taking a view similar to that just advanced and pointing out that for all practical purposes intelligence is to be considered as "a group of innate capacities by virtue of which the individual is capable of learning in a greater or less degree in terms of the amount of these innate capacities with which he is endowed" (130, 17). This view makes intelligence distinct from knowledge, a usage which often leads to misunderstanding and confusion. Ward (135, 115) has perhaps suggested a better usage when he considers intellect to be native capacity, which, with the addition of knowledge constitutes intelligence. However, the modern view will be accepted and intelligence will be considered as distinct from knowledge and from traits of character or temperament.

The next point to be considered is growth of intelligence. It is evident that with the development of the child's brain there comes a change in mental capacity aside from the mere appropriation of knowledge. A child cannot learn integral calculus while many adults can. This represents a vertical growth in intellectual power. It is of course impossible to separate nature and nurture, all that can be done is to hold one variable constant and then make classifications and comparisons to show the effect of the other variable. For example, it could be shown that learning capacity at maturity or later childhood is increased even if there is no training. A child of intelligent parents might be kept out of school through sickness and yet when training was resumed greater learning capacity would be manifested. There is physiological evidence for such a change in that there is a growth of the brain in size up to at least seven years of age and after that it is likely that there is increasing complexity of convolutions and neurone structure. There is evidence that the rate of growth is peculiar to a given individual who will differ from others in this respect even under the same environmental conditions, and furthermore the rate is fairly constant. The final level of arrest also tends to correspond to the rate of growth. This rate of growth is represented by the I.Q., or ratio between mental and chronological age. While capacity at last becomes constant the acquisition of knowledge continues throughout life just as an automobile remains of the same power but its continued performance is registered in milage on the speedometer.

Intelligence can only be known by performance and types of performance suggest that there may be several factors or aspects of intelligence, which like dimensions determine volume. Certainly with growth of intelligence there is increased power, in the sense of increased ability to learn intricate and abstruse material and to perceive complicated and abstract relationships. According to an analogy suggested by Boring (13), this would correspond to the hill climbing capacity of an automobile. It is possible, however, that that performance at a given level of difficulty might vary as to rapidity or speed. This would correspond to the speed of a car as determined for the most part by the gear ratio. Again there are differences as to quality of performance. Learning may be exact and accurate or quite the contrary. By analogy, cars of the same power and speed may differ as to reliability and smoothness of performance. Finally intellectual performance may vary as to versatility. At a given level of difficulty there may be differences between individuals as to range of abilities. This might be illustrated by the all around serviceability of a car, the degree to which it is suited to diverse conditions of roads, weather, types of load, etc. This division and analysis of intelligence into its different aspects might be carried on still further so as to approach a multifocal point of view. There is evidence, however, that abilities along the four lines tend to vary together which gives the concept of general intelligence lying back of them all. The general intelligence of an individual really amounts to an abitrary evaluation of the pattern of his various abilities with respect to the average pattern of special abilities in other members of the group. In conclusion then, general intelligence is the innate capacity fixed with the conjugation of the chromosomes in the original cell, which independently of environment determines the differences and resemblances between individuals in ability to learn; the factors of power, speed, accuracy and versatility all being taken into account.

INTELLIGENCE AND HEREDITY

It is implied in the definition of intelligence that it is hereditary, but it is necessary to consider in greater detail the exact meaning of the word heredity. Confusion often arises from the use of the word in two different ways: First as resemblance based on common descent, and second as the sum of the traits of an individual that are determined by the constitution of the original germ cell. Characteristics arising out of a new combination of genes or a mutation, perhaps due to the dropping out of a chromosome, are certainly innate and yet there may be no resemblance to relatives. The word will be used in the latter rather than the former sense, but still more carefully defined.

Heredity has no meaning save in relation to a particular environment, for even Mendelian traits, as Jennings has shown, either appear or fail to appear depending on environment (71). Furthermore, heredity has no meaning save in relation to the traits of other individuals. The heredity of an individual is simply the constitution of the original cell from which he developed, which would make him differ from other individuals under the same environment, and cause him to resemble other individuals developing from similar cells under different environmental conditions. This is perhaps not the whole story but it is all that we can know. When we have but one individual we do not know which characteristics are due to heredity and which to environment. Likewise, when individuals have origin in different cells and develop under different environments, then we can not tell with assurance the exact cause of their differences, whether it be heredity or environment, nor can we tell the cause of resemblances when the original cells and the environments are both the same. The definition of intelligence that has been given corresponds to this point of view. If all individuals differed widely in both biological origin and training, it would be impossible to know intelligence as such, for there would be a "no man's land," to be claimed by both nature and nurture. Such is not the case, however, and if it can be shown that the range of differences in ability as we know them in society today may still exist in spite of similar environments, and resemblances as we know them may exist under different environments, to that extent differences and resemblances of individuals and groups in ability may be considered as due to intelligence. All investigations of heredity and intelligence directly or indirectly follow this method of studying differences and resemblances that exist independently of, or in spite of environmental conditions.

If it be established that the differences and resemblances in ability can be explained by heredity, a very important conclusion follows, namely, that, in the case of groups, intelligence will not only be hereditary in the sense that was accepted, but also that there will be complete resemblance based on common descent. While the intelligence of an individual will not of necessity be exactly the same as that of the parents, yet in the case of large numbers of individuals, such deviations will cancel one another. (The mental ability of an immigrant group in one generation will be a matter of native intelligence and the average of intelligence will remain the same in the next and following generations in spite of education, save in so far as there is selection.) The next step is to review very briefly the types of evidence that show that differences and resemblances in learning capacity exist independently of environment and training.

1. Analogy between mental and physical differences

The wide variation of individuals as to physical traits cannot be denied and since such traits as stature, eye-color, hair-color, etc., differ widely, even when people develop in the same environment, it must be admitted that these differences are due to heredity. While it is true that the basis of intelligence is physical yet the recognition of similar wide variation in mental traits is recent. The egalitarian view of Ward (134) is rapidly giving way to that of Galton (46), although Boring has raised cogent objections against the acceptance of the Gaussian curve in its exact mathematical form as representing the necessary distribution of mental traits (12). Even if the evidence from mental tests be ignored, there are certainly obvious differences in memory (119, 322), types of imagery (45), and school achievement. The grade location of children of the same age and the same general environment shows great variation (97, 76), and according to Starch (117, 29), in various types of intellectual performance, the best pupil is from two to twenty-five times as able as the poorest pupil in a given group. If variation in physical traits is due to heredity, it would seem that the similar variation in mental traits is due to the same cause since these traits have a physical basis.

2. Correlation of ability of relatives

Karl Pearson and his school have done more than any other group along this line of investigation. The general conclusion is that the correlation between the intelligence of parent and offspring and between siblings is about 0.50, which is very nearly the same correlation as that obtained in the case of physical traits (92).

These findings are significant, but not absolutely conclusive, for it might be argued that the common environment of the relatives had just enough effect to make the correlation equal to that for physical traits. This is rendered unlikely, however, by the fact that but low correlations were found to exist between environmental conditions and intelligence, even when the effect of the various environmental factors were combined by the use of the multiple correlation technique (39). These general conclusions based on estimates of intelligence tend to be confirmed when objective tests are used (40). There is further evidence that environment is not the cause of the resemblances, for Starch found the correlation for siblings to be no greater, when the mental traits tested, were such as seemed likely to be affected by school training (117, 82). Madsen found the same general correlation although his results were a trifle higher (78, 562).

The full measure of heredity, in the sense that we have defined it, is not determined by the correlations between particular relatives, but the method does offer strong indirect evidence. It has a certain value in connection with eugenic selection for it furnishes a measure of predictability, although exact prognosis as to the resemblance of relatives in particular cases is not possible. While an offspring may be more or less intelligent than the parent, yet when a number of cases are considered, plus and minus deviations cancel and the average intelligence of the group remains constant from generation to generation.

3. Resemblances in eminence

Another approach to the problem is to consider the resemblance in eminence among the members of the same family. The method depends in part on an assumption of irrepressibility of genius, and has significance for our purposes only in so far as eminence may be considered as depending on intelligence. Galton, Schuster, Ellis, Jordan, Winship and Woods all present evidence showing that such a resemblance runs in families, but in most cases favorable heredity is accompanied by favorable environment and hence the variables are not controlled as they must be for a conclusive demonstration. The studies do show that, of families of the same environment, certain ones tend to produce eminent representatives. It is only by taking families of the same social class as units that the conditions of constant environment and varied heredity are satisfied. It is of course suggestive that, as Galton pointed out, the adopted nephews of popes were no more eminent than nephews of able men would be expected to be, and that as Woods pointed out, the tendency for eminence to run in families was as great in democratic America as in aristocratic England (136). The latter writer has satisfied the conditions as to control of variables more completely in his study of royalty (137). Here in a constantly favorable environment members of the same family show a correlation as to ability. If environment had been all powerful there could have been no variation and hence no correlation. The study distinctly shows that families taken as units differ markedly in the same favorable environment.

4. Resemblances in degeneracy

There have been many studies in degeneracy that in general follow the same methods as in the studies of eminence and in so doing are open to much the same criticism. In the case of the Jukes, the Hill Folk, the Nams, the Zeros, the Dwellers in the Vale of Siddom, the Smoky Pilgrims, the Tribe of Ishmael, etc., bad heredity and bad environment tend to vary together. In the case of the Kallikak family conditions were better controlled and the descendants were distinctly feebleminded, a state not to be attributed to ordinary environmental conditions (52).

5. Segregation of mental traits

Mental traits that tend to follow Mendelian principles give clear evidence of marked differences in intelligence in spite of an environment that is practically identical for the two or more individuals concerned. A taint of feeble-mindedness may be latent in two parents and then appear as actual mental defect in one of two children, the other being perfectly normal, in spite of the same environment. Such differences can only be explained by differences in the constitution of the germ cells, and since heredity is thus responsible for the very great differences in intelligence that lie between normality and abject feeble-mindedness it can readily explain lesser differences.

6. Studies of twins

A very effective approach to the problem of intelligence and heredity is to be found in the study of twins. Since there are identical and fraternal twins it is possible to investigate the degree to which twins originally different remain so in spite of the common environment, and the degree to which identical twins remain similar even after the respective environments have become different. Galton investigated a considerable number of pairs, using the questionnaire method, and from the permanence of resemblances and differences in spite of environment he concludes, "There is no escape from the conclusion that nature prevails enormously over nurture when the differences of nurture do not exceed what is commonly to be found among persons of the same rank of society and in the same country" (45, 172). Thorndike (127) using tests, found that twins failed to grow more alike with the continuance of a common environment, that they showed more resemblance than siblings also having a common environment, and finally that twins showed no greater resemblance in subjects considered susceptible to training than in others. Gesell (49) has shown the remarkable similarity that may exist between two twins even in details of mental structure. Merriman (82) has recently made a very thorough and convincing study using the modern mental tests. The pairs of like sex, who were of course much more likely to be identical twins, showed a much higher correlation in intelligence scores than the unlike pairs, and since the correlations are about the same at different ages it appears that the length of the period of time they have been subjected to a common environment has little or no effect.

7. The effect of practice

The final, and in many ways the most convincing evidence, is to be found in connection with the effects of practice on differences. It is common knowledge that children are not rendered equal in ability by schooling but rather become separated more widely. Experimental studies lead to the same conclusion. After several investigations Starch concludes, "All experimental results point in the direction that practice does not equalize abilities; in fact, equal practice tends to increase differences in achievement and skill rather than to decrease them. The more gifted individuals profit more, both relatively and absolutely, than the less gifted" (117, 91). The general conclusion from the available evidence, which has been merely outlined here, would seem to be that the great differences that exist in mental ability are really differences in intelligence, that is to say, they are due to heredity.

CAN INTELLIGENCE BE MEASURED?

There still remains the question as to whether or not intelligence can be measured, but to answer this it would be necessary to review the entire testing movement, which is of course impossible here although it has been ably done by Young (142). Undoubtedly there has been undue confidence and enthusiasm, but a more sane and reasonable attitude is being forged in the fire of discussion and controversy. There is a tendency to question normality of distribution of abilities, and since units of test achievement are hardly equal and interchangable as are pounds or feet, it is more appropriate to speak of classification according to intelligence than to speak of its measurement. More important still is the growing conviction that pure native intelligence may not be sifted out automatically from acquired knowledge. There is no such thing as intelligence separated from training, and in most cases learning capacity is tested by what has already been learned. As a rule, the opportunity to acquire the slight amount of knowledge necessary is common to all. Nevertheless, it must be remembered that comparative test scores are not valid indications of comparative intelligence save when a certain minimum of educational opportunity is common to all of the individuals concerned. Likewise, it must be remembered that every test of general intelligence is based on an arbitrary evaluation of factors of power, speed, versatility and accuracy. Intelligence is not homogeneous and a test that is weighted for mechanical ability is likely to give different results from one that is highly verbal and conceptual in type. There is a rough correspondence, however, between the scores on tests of general intelligence, and they meet the important pragmatic test of predicting the limits of achievement under life conditions (128). While the need of control of the environmental factors will be discussed further, given such control it may be accepted that intelligence tests give a rough classification of individuals as to probable achievement in appropriation and advancement of culture, and that the average success of groups in this respect may be quite accurately foretold.

Assuming no great differences in temperament and character, a group of immigrants that on the average make low scores on intelligence tests will tend to be less valuable members of the body politic than others of higher test achievement. They will produce fewer superior individuals, at least if variability be equal, will occupy a lower economic status, will show less acumen in political affairs, and in general will fail to completely participate in a national culture or to greatly advance it.[1]

---

[1] Of course it is not true that traits of personality and temperament are equal, and while of necessity omitted from the present discussion, they could not be ignored in any complete evaluation of immigrant groups. The investigation of such traits has been begun by Davenport (27), McFadden, Dashiell (80), Leaming (76) and others.

CHAPTER II

STUDIES OF IMMIGRANT INTELLIGENCE

METHODS OF STUDY

There has been a steadily growing body of data concerning the intelligence of various immigrant groups and it seems appropriate that this information be brought together, with certain additional data, as a preliminary to presenting the results of the immediate research. No attempt will be made to discuss the work of Ferguson, Mayo, Jordan, Pressey, Pyle, Schwegler, Strong, Derrick, Sunne, and Wells on negro intelligence or the work of Garth and Hunter on that of the Indian, but the summary will be confined to results having a more distinct bearing on trans-oceanic immigration problems. Furthermore no attempt will be made to deal with the theoretical discussion of race differences as such. The term race will either be avoided or used in a popular rather than a strict anthropological sense. There are five ways in which the problem of evaluating immigrant peoples with respect to intelligence may be approached: 1, mental tests, 2, comparative school achievement and grade location, 3, proportion of superior individuals within a given nationality, 4, frequency of mental defect, 5, a study of immigrant case histories, as suggested by Cleghorn (21). Data is available illustrating the first four of these methods. The first is the most promising and will be treated with greater detail.

THE ARMY TESTS

Aside from occasional application of Binet tests to negroes, little progress was made in the study of the comparative mentality of racial and national groups until the development of the Army tests. The difference in achievement on these tests by various national groups has received wide publicity and has been eagerly seized upon as ammunition by many people of prejudiced rather than a scientific turn of mind. Alpha, Beta, and individual examinations were used in the Army testing. Lack of English

15

or an uncertain failure on Alpha caused a soldier to take Beta which might be followed by an individual examination, but the last examination taken was the basis of the final score. "In comparison with the white draft as a whole the foreign-born men required Beta and individual examinations more than twice as frequently as the whole Army group. The high proportion is at least partially explained, of course, by the large foreign-speaking element among the foreign-born" (81, 698). The official report of the Army testing gives the rank order of countries according to the percentage of final letter grades that were D or lower, and also according to the percentage of A and B letter grades (81, 698).

TABLE 1

COUNTRY	PER CENT D, D−, OR E	COUNTRY	PER CENT A OR B
England	8.7	England	19.7
Holland	9.2	Scotland	13.0
Denmark	13.4	White draft	12.1
Scotland	13.6	Holland	10.7
Germany	15.0	Canada	10.5
Sweden	19.4	Germany	8.3
Canada	19.5	Denmark	5.4
Belgium	24.0	Sweden	4.3
White draft	24.1	Norway	4.1
Norway	25.6	Ireland	4.1
Austria	37.5	All foreign	4.0
Ireland	39.4	Turkey	3.4
Turkey	42.0	Austria	3.4
Greece	43.6	Russia	2.7
All foreign	45.6	Greece	2.1
Russia	60.4	Italy	0.8
Italy	63.4	Belgium	0.8
Poland	69.9	Poland	0.5

It is apparent that there are very considerable differences, but not all of the figures are significant in view of the small number of representatives from certain countries such as Holland and Belgium. The total number of foreign-born, however, was well over ten thousand and Brigham has taken this data and worked it over, using a combined scale that reduced the scores of the Alpha, Beta, and individual tests to common terms. He then calculates the probable errors of the differences in score between the various groups and thus checks the adequacy of the samples. The combined scale runs from 0 to 25 and the nationalities made average scores as indicated in table 2 (15, 124). Space does not permit a detailed presentation of the validity of the differences, as determined by the size of the probable errors worked out by Brigham, but the following facts stand out: 1, The English-speaking countries, with the exception of Ireland rank highest in intelligence and exceed the white draft taken as a whole; 2, the non-English-speaking countries of Northern Europe also make a good showing; 3, the Slavic countries such as Russia and Poland and the Mediterranean countries such as Italy make a very poor record; 4, the native-born do better than the foreign-born

TABLE 2

United States officers	18.84	Belgium	12.79
England	14.87	Ireland	12.32
Scotland	14.34	Austria	12.27
Holland	14.32	Turkey	12.02
Germany	13.88	Greece	11.90
United States white draft	13.77	Russia	11.34
Denmark	13.69	Italy	11.01
Sweden	13.30	Poland	10.74
Norway	12.98	United States colored	10.41

taken as a whole, for 74.8 per cent of the native-born exceed the average of the foreign-born. Their average on the combined scale is 13.77 as compared with 12.05. The difference of 1.72 is 92 times its probable error of 0.0186; 5, the final important fact, brought out by the Army report and elaborated by Brigham, is the steady decline in scores when the 11,295 foreign-born are divided up into five year residence groups. Those who have been here from 0 to 5 years have an average score of 11.41 while those who have been here twenty years or more exceed the native-born with a score of 13.82. The increase of scores with successive age groups is, in most cases, statistically significant (15, 91).

INTERPRETATIONS.

1. It may be held with Brigham that the scores made on the tests by the various national groups correspond to the proportion

of Nordic blood, and that the lower scores of recent immigrants
is due, at least in part, to their smaller proportion of Nordic
stock.   2. There may have been unfair sampling of the population
in this country.   3. The national and racial groups in this country
may not have been fair representatives of the respective races or
nationalities taken as a whole.   4. There may have been a return
of less successful immigrants who were also less intelligent, and
this may have taken place to a different extent among the various
nationalities.   5. To explain the differential achievement of the
residence groups it might be suggested that younger boys would
have to be brighter in order to venture emigration or to have their
parents aid them in so doing.[1]   6. The national groups and
residence groups may have had their score determined by degree of
Americanization.   7. The results hinge not so much upon a so-
called Americanization process as upon education and linguistic
facility.

The first interpretation, in so far as it is based on a hypothesis
of Nordic superiority, must be considered of very doubtful worth.
It has been ably criticized by Young (143), Bagley (6) and others.
The second explanation is probably not very important, for the
nature of the selection and facts as to the composition of the army
make it likely that both nationality and residence groups were
fairly represented.   The third point is of significance, but while
it rules out sweeping generalizations such as implied in the first
interpretation, yet it is hardly a complete explanation.   The next
two interpretations simply suggest mechanisms which might
bring about the differential selective influence.   The final two
interpretations together with the third go to the roots of the
matter.   There are some traits, either native or acquired, which
characterize the older residence groups and representatives from
Northern Europe, that make for superior achievement on the
tests.   The matter reduces itself to the problem of evaluating
the relative effect of heredity and environment as determining
the test scores.

[1] A review of Brigham's book by E. G. Boring, Facts and Fancies of
Immigration, *New Republic*, April 25, 1923, pp. 245–46, mentions this point.

TEST SCORES AND ENVIRONMENT

To attribute an influence on test results to education is to question the claim that the test measured native intelligence independent of language and training. There is no such thing as a test that is independent of acquired experience, it is merely a question whether the differences in environmental background that existed in the case of the groups tested were sufficient to affect the results. When there are two variables that might affect a third, in order to attribute the result to one independent variable, the other must either be kept constant or else shown to be of no effect. Brigham rules out the language and Americanization factors by comparing the relative increase of Alpha and Beta scores with longer residence, and certainly this is a very fundamental point, for it would be expected that Alpha scores would increase more than Beta scores under the influence of the American environment. However, even if the increase were uniform there is some possibility that both were effected by favorable environment to a certain extent. In general the improvement is almost as great on Beta as on Alpha (15, 102) although Hexter and Myerson (64) vigorously denounce Brigham for misinterpreting the figures. These reviewers claim that the speed factor was a handicap to the foreign-born and they criticize Brigham for not giving the probable error when he meets this objection by showing a high correlation of the tests when given with single and with double time.

Further research is throwing light on the degree to which the tests warrant the conclusions that have been drawn from the results of their application. As to the influence of alleged speed factor, which perhaps would bear more severely on those with an unfavorable environment, Ruch (110) cites a study of 510 cases indicating a correlation of 0.965 between the scores for single and double time. While the absolute scores were raised, the rank order was unchanged. He argues that the effects of practice are consistent with initial results, and that the limits are really so fixed that all of the material within the individual's capacity can be completed within the allotted time. A second study (109) confirms the results of the first. The Alpha tests were given to

122 freshmen at a state university. The scores for single time were found to correlate to the extent of 0.966 with those for double time and to the extent of 0.945 with the scores for unlimited time. Dull subjects do not equal the scores of the bright students, and the mean of their scores for unlimited time is below the mean of the high group for single time. The latter, however, were too near the upper limit of the scale to determine whether the differences increased. When the total scores are considered, there is no increase in the amount of overlapping of the high and low groups when the time allowance is increased. The general conclusion that he draws is that the Army tests are to be considered validated, as something more than mere tests of mental agility.

Dunlap and Snyder (38) have also experimented with the Alpha tests, especially in connection with the effects of practice. College seniors showed striking improvement on the second and third trials and the practice effect for the lower half of the group was especially great, perhaps indicating that the novelty factor was more significant for those making low scores than for those of superior performance. Davidson says,

Sympathizers with those psychologists who contend that differences in the power to learn, to acquire, or to improve by practice, are the really substantial differences among individuals, will hesitate to accept indices of native capacity derived from single performances where the antecedent practice is essentially unknown. It is just in this inequality of practice in all exercises highly subject to training that the experience of the several social levels is most unlike, with the obvious consequence that the lower or comparatively unschooled classes suffer from an undue depression of their scores in such exercises (28, 187–188).

Davidson not only questions the isolation of innate ability and the validity of the samples, but after citing the low correlation of 0.40 or 0.50 between test scores and school achievement, raises the question as to whether the test results really indicate social value. There is a correlation of about 0.75 between the scores on the Alpha test and the number of years schooling of the soldier, and a coefficient, a trifle smaller between Beta scores and schooling. This is cited by both the proponents and the opponents of the tests to support their views. Brigham claims that levels of ability are indicated by school elimination while others claim that schooling determined the scores on the test.

There is additional evidence concerning the problem of the influence of education and experience. The doctors, engineers and other officers seemed to show an achievement profile on the subtests corresponding to their special training. The engineers, for example, were rather superior where mathematics was involved. Bishop (10) has made some very significant experiments in this connection. He arranged similar groups, paired as to age, sex, etc., and then gave one group practice in the principles involved in one part of the test and the other group similar indirect practice in another part of the test. A tremendous increase in score, on the material receiving indirect practice over the unpracticed part of the test, resulted in the case of both groups, in spite of the fact that nothing was taught that would not have been acquired in a favorable environment.

None of the critics of the tests have argued more vigorously against assumed measurement of purely native intelligence than Bagley (5). He has carried on the work of Alexander (1) and Pintner (93) in correlating the median score of representatives of various states with economic and social conditions. Alexander found a correlation of 0.72 P.E. 0.05 between the median Alpha scores of the men, from the forty-one states that were adequately represented, and the rating of the states on the Ayres scale of school efficiency. Bagley points out that the states of Oregon and Washington which stood high on Alpha, but lower in school efficiency, had new comers who came from states that ranked high in school efficiency. Taking only the states that had 55 per cent of the population born in the state, in order to eliminate the effect of population movements, the correlation was raised to 0.82. He argues that the correlation is not due to inheritance of the intelligence that created the school efficiency, since the negro median scores show a closer relation to school efficiency than do the white scores. He holds it improbable that the negroes would select states of residence in such a fashion as to almost exactly match their intelligence with school efficiency. It is also pointed out that the Beta test does not show as great a correlation with education as Alpha and hence one or the other fails to measure innate intelligence. Bagley also refers to the application of the partial correlation method by Burt (18) showing the Binet tests are affected by native intelligence to the extent of 33 per cent, by general experience 11 per cent, and by formal schooling 54 per cent. It is not likely that the Alpha test is much more independent of environment than is the Stanford-Binet test, and yet Gordon (57), another English psychologist, has shown that extreme environmental handicaps, such as experienced by Gypsy children, children living in canal boats, and those suffering from physical defects, do affect the score. Older children regularly show a lower I.Q. than the younger children in the same family, apparently due to the continued influence of environmental handicaps, especially inadequate schooling.

In a recent article, Bagley (6) has followed up his study of the relationship between school conditions in various states and the test achievement of those subjected to those conditions by correlating the ranking of the various European countries in educational status with the average test achievement of their representatives in the American Army. He finds a correlation of 0.84, but the question as to which variable is the cause and which is the effect still remains unanswered.

There is an approach to the problem that supports rather strongly the view that the Army tests really demonstrated significant innate differences between nationality groups. Since few would deny that distinct mental defect is in most cases due to heredity rather than lack of education, if it be found that frequency of mental defect in various groups is associated with a low standing as determined by mental tests, the most reasonable implication would be that the tests really measured in a rough way the innate abilities of the various groups. The writer correlated the median Alpha scores for the different states, as worked out by Alexander and quoted by Bagley (5), with the frequency of mental defect among the soldiers having residence in the various states. The data on mental defect was worked over from that collected by Bailey and Haber, which will be described in greater detail in another connection. Since only the absolute numbers of feeble-minded from the various states were given, it was necessary to divide by the number of males in each state between the ages of 20 and 44, the results being expressed in terms of the number of feeble-minded soldiers per hundred thousand of the state populations of this age and sex. Using the rank order method, the result of the correlation was a negative coefficient −0.76 which, when translated into terms of the Pearson r amounted to −0.78 P.E. 0.046. Another method of expressing the tendency to mental defect among the representatives of the various states consisted in determining the percent of the total number of neuropsychiatric cases from a given state that were feeble-minded, and using that percentage as an index. When the percentage of feeble-minded among the neuropsychiatric cases was correlated against the median Alpha scores for the various states, a negative coefficient of −0.72 was obtained, which converted into a Pearson r of −0.74 P.E. 0.047 or about the same value obtained by the other method. The two indices of the tendency to mental defect correlated very decidedly with each other, yielding on conversion a r of 0.84 P.E. 0.026. The negative coefficients of −0.78 and −0.74 mean that a marked relationship exists between low scores on mental tests and high incidence of mental defect. Since the latter is due to heredity and is correlated with the former, it is likely that the average scores of the groups on mental tests are also largely determined by innate capacity, all of which renders more significant the differences in test achievement between the various racial and national groups in this country.

It is not claimed, however, that this evidence is conclusive. Even Brigham is forced to admit superiority in test achievement of the English-speaking members over others of the same race, which fact must be explained before education and language are ruled out. Until the range of variation in environment that leaves test results unaffected is worked out, group comparisons by means of tests must be considered valid only in proportion as the environmental conditions are kept constant. The Army data must be regarded as suggestive but not conclusive, and we must look for further evidence in studies of the children of immigrants who have had a fairly equal background of opportunity in the schools. Partial summaries of such studies have been made by Pintner (96) and Young (144) but it seems worth while to bring them together as completely as possible in order to make possible comparisons with the Army results and with the findings of the research carried on by the writer.

Brown has given the Stanford-Binet tests to samples of children from various nationalities in Michigan. This test was used rather than a group test because of the language difficulties in the lower grades. This difficulty was not found throughout, however. "In other words, it was found that after a pupil had attended an American school for one or two years, he tested as high by employing the English language as by using his native tongue" (16, 324). The results are given below in table 3. The

TABLE 3

NATIONALITY	NUMBER OF CASES	MEDIAN I.Q.
Norwegian.....................................	34	103.75
German...	67	102.3
Swedish..	187	101.9
English...	90	101.75
Austrian.......................................	28	99.5
French...	199	95.4
Finnish...	226	90.0
Slovak...	31	85.6
Italian...	51	77.5

favorable showing of the children of North European ancestry and the striking inferiority of the Italians is in accord with the Army findings.

<h2>MURDOCK'S STUDY</h2>

Miss Katherine Murdock (85) has made a study of the intelligence of certain national groups in New York. The Jews, negroes and white Americans were unselected but the Italians were picked from those having no language handicap according to the opinion of the teacher. The social and economic status was very much the same for all of the groups, and the numbers ample, several hundred of each nationality being tested. The Pressey Group Test was used, the results being expressed in terms of the number of points scored. Children 9 to 16 years of age were dealt with and at most ages the Jews and American children were about equal and both superior to the Italians and negroes, while up to, and including the age of 13, the negroes were superior to the Italians, and were inferior only at ages 14 and 16. The results are readily summed up by stating the percentages exceeding the median of the Jewish group. In the case of the Italian children the average percentage exceeding the median of the Jews for age groups 11, 12 and 13, was 15.5 per cent. In the case of the Americans for the same ages the average percentage superior to the Jews was 53.66 per cent and in the case of the negroes 30.33 per cent. The poor showing of the Italians is striking in view of the fact that only those who had no language handicap were tested.

FEINGOLD'S STUDY

Feingold (41) made a study at Hartford High School to find out whether the mental differences among the racial groups of the first generation are as great as among the original immigrants, and also to investigate the mental status of the Jewish youth. He criticizes the exponents of the Army results by pointing out that no account was taken of the varied European environments, and maintains that, since the later immigrants are related to the earlier, to suppose that a change has occurred with five-year residence groups is to suppose that a change has taken place in the level of intelligence in Europe, which is absurd. It is rather hard to see the absurdity of this in view of a very possible change in selective forces. Feingold very properly feels that it would be of value to make a study in which the factors of foreign birth and upbringing were eliminated.

A modified form of the Alpha was given to the senior, junior and freshman classes and the scores for the last two classes were converted into I.Q'S. using Miss Cobb's conversion table. The relative rank of the various groups is presented in table 4. The differences between the various foreign groups compared with each other and with the Americans are rather clear, also the rank order is very nearly the same for the different classes and table 5 shows the marked correspondence with the ranking of the various nationalities on the Army tests.

Feingold is not content to accept intelligence as being of exclusive importance among psychological traits, with respect to which races may differ. Tenacity, will power and persistence he feels should also have a place. He attempts to evaluate such

TABLE 4

NATIONALITY	FRESHMEN		JUNIORS		SENIORS		
	I.Q.	Number	I.Q.	Number	I.Q.	Score	Number
English and Scotch........	105	76	109	17	103	142	19
American..................	103	892	107	286	100	136	264
Jewish....................	103	518	103	208	96	125	146
German...................	103	86	105	20	99	139	13
Dane and Swede..........	102	114	101	28	98	131	30
French...................	98	35		6			6
Irish.....................	98	278	100	44	97	125	53
Polish....................	97	90	101	11	92	117	11
Italian...................	97	206	100	29	96	118	16
Colored..................	95	58	94	15	91	121	9
Average..................	102	2,353	103	664	98	130	567

TABLE 5

ARMY	FRESHMEN	THREE CLASSES COMBINED
1. English	1. English and Scotch	1. English and Scotch
2. Scotch	2. American	2. American
3. American	3. Jewish	3. German
4. German	4. German	4. Jewish
5. Danish	5. Danish and Swedish	5. Danish and Swedish
6. Swedish	6. French	6. French
7. Irish	7. Irish	7. Irish
8. Italian	8. Italian	8. Polish
9. Polish	9. Polish	9. Italian
10. Colored	10. Colored	10. Colored

traits by ratios of intellectual to academic standing, and finds that when mental levels are equal, as shown by tests, the Jews make a very much superior showing in academic achievement. Grier (61), however, found that Jewish boys were inferior in school standing to the Americans up to the age of 16, although the girls were superior to the Americans at most ages.

For our purposes, however, the results of the intelligence tests are of chief importance. While the study is admirable in that by taking older children it reduces the language factor to a minimum, yet there is a weakness due to the possibility of selection. It is not likely that the same proportion of different nationalities as found in the grammar school continues in the high school. It would certainly be expected that only the better elements of the foreign population continue their school career, and being thus selected tend to compare more favorably with the comparatively unselected Americans. This possibility is somewhat opposed by the fact that, with advancement in high school, the differences between the groups standing high and those of low rank fail to decrease. Feingold is inclined to think that it is due to the handicap of race discrimination rather than to different levels of mental arrest.

BERRY'S REPORT ON TESTING IN DETROIT

The report of C. S. Berry on the testing of some ten thousand first grade pupils in Detroit by the Detroit First Grade Intelligence Test gives some very interesting results (9). The point ratings were changed into letter grades ranging from A to E but these were further condensed for purposes of classification to grades of Z, Y and X. Group X consisted of A and B pupils who comprised the upper 22.4 per cent of the entire body of ten thousand or more first grade pupils. Y included the C+ and C and the C— pupils and embraced the middle 60.5 per cent of the total. The Z group included the D and E pupils and was made up of the lower 17.1 per cent of the total. The grade location of the children according to the birth place of the father is shown in table 6 (9, 14).

The striking thing is the low scores made by the Polish and Italian children while, as in other studies, the children of English and Canadian parentage rank with the American. If it be argued that language difficulties were the cause, it still remains to be explained why the Germans and Russians did so much better than the Italians. When a classification was made of the basis of the language spoken in the home, for those speaking Polish, the results were about the same since almost all of the Poles spoke Polish in the home.

Most of the Russians spoke Yiddish so that the achievement of the Yiddish-speaking group is practically that of the children of Russian born fathers. Likewise almost all of the Italians spoke Italian, but in the case of the Germans only about 60 per cent came from homes where German was spoken. Evidently the Germans learn English more readily or have been in this country for a longer time. There is undoubtedly a certain language handicap suggested by the fact that the children of German parentage have 25 per cent in the X group and 12 per cent in the Z group, while those that speak German in the home

TABLE 6

BIRTHPLACE OF FATHER	GROUP X	GROUP Y	GROUP Z	NUMBER OF CASES	TOTAL
	per cent	per cent	per cent		per cent
England	29.9	62.0	8.2	218	2.1
Canada	29.6	61.2	9.2	431	4.2
United States	28.7	60.3	11.0	5,272	51.2
Germany	25.2	63.2	11.6	318	3.1
Hungary	20.9	59.1	20.0	340	3.1
Russia	15.4	63.0	21.6	707	6.9
Poland	9.0	54.4	36.6	1,222	11.9
Italy	6.1	55.9	38.0	679	6.6
Other countries	16.1	59.1	24.8	1,111	10.9
Total	22.1	59.5	18.2	10,298	100.0

have only 17 per cent in the X group and 19 per cent in the Z group. Either there is a language handicap, or else the parents who fail to acquire the use of English are less intelligent, and pass on their dullness to their children. The important thing, however, is that the Germans still rank far above the Italians, and while certainly speaking Yiddish is as great a handicap as speaking Italian, yet those speaking Yiddish have twice as large a percentage in the X group and less than one half as large a percent in the Z group. Furthermore Berry says, "Of the groups coming from homes where a foreign language is spoken the Jews not only test the highest, but have the largest percent completing semester's work and largest percent of promotions. The

Italians, on the other hand, test lowest, have the smallest percent of promotions, and have next to the lowest percent completing a semester's work" (9, 16). The low standing of the Italians is confirmed by Miss Bere who found the average I.Q. for a 100 Italian children to be only 83 (96).

YOUNG'S STUDY

Young (145) has made one of the most scientific and complete studies that has yet been worked out. His purpose was to investigate the mental differences in certain immigrant groups and to consider the matter of an alleged language handicap. The survey was made in California, where "Latin" groups, consisting of South Italians, Portuguese and Spanish Mexicans were compared with children of North European ancestry. All of the children were 12 years of age and in addition to scores on Alpha and Beta tests, grade location, teachers' estimates of intelligence, and estimates of school work were obtained. With groups of constant age, grade location is of course very significant. The modal grade for the non-Latin children was the low seventh, for the South Italians, the high fifth, for the Spanish-Mexicans the high fourth, and for the Portuguese the fifth. The teachers' estimates, which were given on a scale of seven, showed the Italians to be on the average 0.8 of one class rank below the Americans. The Portuguese were over a class rank below and the Spanish-Mexicans were over one and a quarter class ranks below. While social status differed in favor of the Americans, no very high correlation was found with individual intelligence scores. The general results of the study are shown in table 7, which Young prepared from a larger table in his original study, by omitting a miscellaneous group of Americans and a miscellaneous group of Italians which show the same relationships as the main groups. The numbers of cases tested were omitted from the summary article in the *Scientific Monthly*, but are added here from the data in the original monograph.

If the results be put into terms of percentage exceeding the median of the Americans, the change places the nationalities in the same order save that in the case of Alpha the positions of the Portuguese and the Spanish-Mexicans are reversed. It is apparent that the differences are very considerable on the Alpha tests, and that on the Beta, the Americans are still much superior, although the other groups make relatively a better showing. The facts suggest a language handicap on Alpha, when applied to groups of children of foreign descent, but Young is not inclined to accept this conclusion. He points out that higher thought processes are bound up with the use of symbols, and that the so called verbal tests investigate intellectual power rather than mere verbal fluency. While the Latins had a considerable percentage of zero scores on certain of the verbal elements of the Alpha test, yet it was high for all of the children, only relatively greater for the Latins than the Americans (145, 58). The Latins also made a good many zero scores on non-verbal sub-tests. In general, according to Young, an analysis of the sub-tests failed to demonstrate a relationship between the achievement of the

TABLE 7

RACE GROUP	NUMBER OF CASES	MEDIAN ALPHA	P.E. DIST.	MEDIAN BETA	P.E. DIST.
American....................	314	59.21	18.48	68.88	7.03
Italian.....................	191	24.92	13.90	54.75	10 90
Portuguese.................	77	22.00	15.65	52.03	9.88
Spanish-Mexican............	51	23.67	12.82	52.96	10.76

Latins and the amount of language facility required on the various sub-tests.

It is claimed that the Beta test was not well adapted to the Americans, lacking discrimination and a sufficient range, thus lowering the differences between these children and the Italians. In general the contention is that the comparatively inferior performance of the foreign groups arises out of a lack of conceptual intelligence or in other words of intellectual power, rather than from a language handicap. Much stress is laid on the high correlation of Alpha with school grade and school achievement, even for the Latins which it is claimed demonstrates the validity of the tests. "The up-shot of the whole matter is that the alleged language handicap of the Latins simply does not exist to the extent imagined" (145, 59). Pintner criticizes the argument from correlations rather effectively. "But we should not forget that a teacher's estimate of a child's intelligence will unquestionably be influenced by the child's ability to use the English language, and, of course, all the child's schoolwork is conditioned by his ability to understand and make use of English" (95, 292). The question of prognosis for school purposes must not be confused with the question of the absolute intelligence of different racial groups.

Other studies have been made dealing with subjects of the same general racial type in the same locality. Dickson (37) studied first grade children in California and obtained the results

TABLE 8

Differences in I.Q. of first graders by racial stock

RACE	NUMBER OF CASES	MEDIAN I.Q.
Spanish................................	37	78
Italian (chiefly Southern Italians).............	25	84
Portuguese................................	23	84
Northern-European born....................	14	105
American (Northern-European ancestry).......	49	106

TABLE 9

RACE	1916 MEDIAN I.Q.	1920 MEDIAN I.Q.
Total South European......................	88.0	85.5
Portuguese................................	88.3	74.0
Americans (from one school).................	111.0	110.5
Americans (from second school)..............	102.3	95.0

shown in table 8. It might be argued that the low achievement of the Latins on the Stanford-Binet test was due to environmental handicaps to be overcome by equal school advantages. In order to test such a possibility, Miss Thompson (125) tested many of the same children five years later, which period of time would be expected to wipe out handicaps of language and of family background. The results are shown in table 9 and it is apparent that no improvement has taken place. Only about two thirds of the original group of children could be found, but moving away would hardly be expected to bring about any definite selection, and her study must be considered as weighty evidence tending to minimize the importance of the language factor. Additional data of her own showed the same decided superiority of the children of North European ancestry.

This evidence indicating the slight effect of continued schooling, is supported by data from Madsen (78) who found that 16 Italian children had an average I.Q. of 80.1, when retested with the Stanford-Binet tests, as compared with 79.3 at the time of entrance a year and a half earlier.

WORK OF PASCHAL AND SULLIVAN

A study of physical and mental traits of Mexican children has a certain amount of relevant material. Several hundred children were tested in Tucson, Arizona, comprising all of the nine year olds and all of the twelve year olds in the schools. There were a hundred in each age and sex group making four hundred in all. There was a slight correlation of score with skin color. The children born in Mexico made better scores on the six individual performance tests than did those born in Tucson, which is reassuring as to the quality of recent immigration, and tends to rule out the language factor. A comparison with American norms shows an overlapping on the upper half of the distributions but from the median down the American children show an increasing superiority. The inferiority as compared with the American children was greater at 9 years than at 12, which was held to show the effect of schooling on the mental growth of the twelve year olds (90).[2]

WORK OF PINTNER AND KELLER

Pintner has engaged in two studies with the purpose of determining the effect of language in race comparisons and incidently data of a comparative nature is given. The first study (94) was made at Youngstown, Ohio, in order to determine the influence

---

[2] A more recent study made by Sheldon (114) of a hundred Mexican and a hundred American children using Stanford-Binet and Cole-Vincent tests showed that the superiority of the Americans increased with chronological age. The average I.Q. was 104.8 as compared with 89 for the Mexicans. The writer concludes that while the Mexicans rank above the Indians they have but 85 per cent of the intelligence of whites.

of language on the Binet test. Cards were sent home to the parents in order to obtain data as to nationality. The results are shown in tables 10 and 11. If the English-speaking and foreign-speaking be compared by schools the results are the same as if the schools are combined. The results will be given in the latter form.

The Pintner Non-Language Test was given to the children of the second grade in one of the schools, with the results shown in table 12. In addition, a group of clinic cases were given Stanford-Binet tests and performance tests, which correlated to the extent of 0.64 in the English speaking group, and only 0.48 for the foreign-speaking children. For the English-speaking group the difference in mental age on the performance as compared with the Stanford-Binet test was only six months, while for the foreign-speaking it was sixteen months. Furthermore 75 per cent of the cases were higher on the performance test, while in the case of the English-speaking group only 52 per cent of the cases stood higher on the performance test. Pintner concludes "that when classified according to mental age, those children who hear a foreign language in their homes may suffer a serious handicap when tested only by the revisions of the Binet Test" (94, 222). These results are rather impressive as showing the influence of the language factor, although it might be argued that the non-language or performance tests did not permit expression of the higher mental processes in which, perhaps, the Americans were superior. It may be that ditch diggers would approach the achievement of college professors on a test of mechanical ability. It should also be noted that the foreign groups did not equal the American's performance even on the non-language test.

The second study made by Pintner for the same purpose was carried on in New York, and dealt with American children, largely of Irish descent, and with Italians, Germans and Polish children. The tests used were the National Intelligence Test, Scale A, Form 1, which is rather verbal in type, and the Pintner Non-Language Test, the results being very similar to those from the first study. They can best be given, as is done in table 13, in terms of the percentage of the foreign group reaching or exceeding the median mental age of the Americans. Here again there

TABLE 10

ENGLISH-SPEAKING			FOREIGN-SPEAKING		
Number of cases	Nationality	I.Q.	Number of cases	Nationality	I.Q.
249	American white	95	313	Italian	84
71	American colored	88	130	Slavish	85
24	English	97	99	Hungarian	89
3	Canadian	89	37	German	91
8	Scotch	88	18	Roumanian	97
5	Irish	92	12	Greek	83
7	Welsh	93	11	Polish	85
			4	Finnish	94

Other nationalities occur in numbers too small to be mentioned.

TABLE 11

	NUMBER	I.Q.	
		Average	Median
English-speaking............................	367	92	94
Foreign-speaking............................	674	84	85

TABLE 12

	CASES	BINET I.Q.	PINTNER I.Q.	GAIN
English-speaking..................	49	99	109	10
Foreign-speaking..................	56	89	103	14

TABLE 13

NATIONALITY	NUMBER OF CASES	PER CENT EXCEEDING MEDIAN OF AMERICANS ON PINTNER TEST	PER CENT EXCEEDING MEDIAN OF AMERICANS ON NATIONAL INTELLIGENCE TEST
German............................	45	62	36
Polish............................	18	61	41
Italian............................	102	43	36
Total foreign....................	165	50	37

seems to be some handicap of language but the Italians, as in most of the studies, are inferior on both tests. The data are not very satisfactory since the numbers are small and as no mention is made of the age of the different groups we can merely infer that they were roughly of the same age since they were all in the third and fourth grades.

<h2 style="text-align:center">ARLITT'S STUDY</h2>

A study by Arlitt (2) has as its primary object the determination of the effect of social status on test scores, but also gives considerable data bearing on comparative racial intelligence. There were 342 children studied in the primary grades of a single district. The 191 children of native-born white parents were separated into five social classes according to the occupation of the parents and it was found that the median I.Q.'s for the social classes from low to high, were 92, 107, 118.7 and 125.9. Taken together the median I.Q. was 106.5, while that of 87 Italians was 85 and that of 71 negroes was 83.4. However, 37 per cent of the native whites came from a superior or very superior social status, while 93 per cent of the negroes and 90 per cent of the Italians came from families of inferior or very inferior social status. If this factor is equalized by comparing the Americans of inferior social status with the other races the median of 92 is only 7 points above the Italians' median and 8.6 above that of the negro. The variation due to race is only 8.6 as over against 33.9 due to social status and hence, according to the conclusion of Miss Arlitt, the latter should be taken into account in determining race norms. It is quite true that it should be taken into account and yet undoubtedly there is a common factor of hereditary capacity lying back of both social status of the family and the intelligence of the children. To compare only groups having the same social status is to compare special samples of the respective racial groups, which may not give a fair picture of the racial groups as a whole. The inferior of one race may be compared with the superior of another thus lessening the difference that would be fonnd to exist between fair samples of the two groups.

CLEVELAND CLINICAL DATA

A study of nationality and mental levels in Cleveland, has recently been reported by Miss Bertha Luckey[3] which yields some interesting comparisons. Some 14,000 children tested at the clinic have been classified by I.Q. and nationality, and while those tested tended to be either sub-normals or super-normals thus causing bimodal distributions, comparisons are valid in so far as the selective forces bringing children to the clinic operated equally on all nationalities. In general the American and Jewish children showed a distinctly higher central tendency. This is closely approached by the Bohemian children who rank somewhat above various groups of children of central and eastern European ancestry. The Italians and negroes rank lowest of all. An interesting point in this connection is the fact that different selective influences operated to bring the immigrant groups to this country. While in the case of certain of the Slavic groups such as the Poles whole villages were more or less directly imported for work in the Cleveland industries, many of the Bohemians emigrated for social or political reasons. In view of such facts, together with the relationship between intelligence and social status demonstrated by Miss Arlitt, the possibility of selection must constantly be kept in mind. As has already been suggested, one interpretation of the Army tests results may be the possibility of a differential selection by social status operating in time and space. We cannot reason from the qualities of immigrants in this country to the qualities of national populations abroad and much less to qualities of races taken as a whole. It is even quite possible that within this country immigrant groups of the same nationality may differ considerably in innate traits due to selective influences.

OTHER STUDIES

Since there is no intention of dealing with the broad problem of race differences, using race in a strict anthropological sense, and since the data is decidedly fragmentary and inconclusive, no

[3] Reported before Section K of the A. A. A. S., January 1, 1925, at the meetings held in Washington.

attempt will be made to present in any detail the studies of the mentality of Oriental peoples. Pyle (101) was one of the first to investigate the intelligence of the Chinese, and from an application of tests to about 500 individuals concluded that their efficiency was considerably less than that of Americans. Murdock (86) finds evidence that seems to indicate that the Anglo-Saxons probably excel the Orientals, including the Chinese. Symonds finds that the results depend on the type of test used and says, "We had better cast away our old blanket concept of racial superiorities and consider superiority rather in terms of separate functions or groups of functions" (120, 442).

The work of Walcott (133) is very inconclusive, but that of Yeung (140) in investigating Chinese children in the vicinity of San Francisco shows that the median I.Q. of these children is but little below the norm for Americans. Porteus (98) presents evidence both from brain capacity and intelligence tests showing that the Japanese approach the level of the Anglo-Saxons and are superior to the Chinese. Fukuda (44) found that a limited number of Japanese children tested but slightly below the American norm. From a study of 7000 children in Hawaii Smith is inclined to think that the inferiority of the Orientals to the whites is largely due to lack of opportunity.[4]

The matter of Oriental intelligence is still very much of an open question but the studies of the intelligence of the children of European immigrant groups, with which we are chiefly concerned, seem to indicate that the stock of the older immigration from northern Europe tends to be superior in test achievement to certain groups of the newer immigration, to an extent that can hardly be explained entirely by environmental factors. It remains to be seen whether this same tendency is shown according to other criteria of intelligence.

NATIONALITY AND SCHOOL PROGRESS

The success of a child in the school is not a perfect criterion for estimating his intelligence, but when large numbers are con-

[4] Paper delivered by Stevenson Smith in connection with Program A of the American Psychological Association dealing with Social and Racial Psychology on December 31, 1924, at Washington.

sidered under controlled environmental conditions the effects of individual temperamental differences tend to cancel out. Hence, differences in the average school achievement of groups suggest differences in average intelligence.

There is but little data concerning comparative achievement of nationalities in the schools in spite of the great importance of a knowledge of such facts for school policy. Jordan (73), however, has made a study in St. Paul and Minneapolis of school progress as related to nationality. These cities were selected because of fairly equal numbers of native-born, native-born of foreign parentage, and foreign-born in the population, and because the

TABLE 14

GROUP	TOTAL CASES	PER CENT RETARDED	RANK	PER CENT ACCELER- ATED	RANK
Roumanian Jew..............	99	24.2	1	51.5	1
United States................	350	32.0	2	38.8	3
Great Britain.................	165	35.1	3	30.9	8
Sweden......................	420	41.2	4	34.5	5
Germany....................	177	42.9	5	37.8	4
Russian Jew.................	336	45.5	6	30.3	9
Austria-Hungary............	129	48.8	7	20.9	11
Finland.....................	45	48.8	8	33.3	6
Norway.....................	215	49.7	9	25.6	10
Denmark....................	22	50.0	10	40.9	2
Poland......................	38	55.2	11	13.2	12
Italy.......................	18	61.1	12	33.3	7

various nationalities were so distributed throughout the cities as to make the school conditions fairly equal. He found the ancestry of the children to be very much mixed but made a classification on the basis of preponderance of one stock over the others. His results as to school progress are presented in table 14.

It is apparent that there is no very marked correlation between low percentage of retardation and high percentage of acceleration. In general the children of American stock and those of northwest Europe make a slightly more favorable showing than the others, although the standing of the Roumanian Jews clearly makes any sweeping generalization to that effect impossible. Data from school marks and intelligence tests tend to be in favor of the

American children.   Jordan denies, however, that innate capacity varies with nationality groups and seeks to explain the differences by an alleged language handicap.   While this may have played a part his analysis does not eliminate the hypothesis of innate differences, nor does it definitely connect facts as to the language used with difficulties in school progress.

The Immigration Commission of 1910 collected a vast amount of data concerning the children of immigrants in the schools (104, 3), which has received little attention but which is worthy and susceptible of analysis.   The number of cases dealt with is far greater than in Jordan's study and are more representative of the country at large, furthermore, it is possible to control many of the factors involved.   The report covers over two million children and 37 cities, with few exceptions, the largest in the country.   The classification is made by race or people following the practice of the Bureau of Immigration, and the children are grouped according to the race or nativity of their fathers.   In the report, retardation is considered to mean an age at least two years greater than that normal for a given grade.   The large sample covering nearly two million children in all of the 37 cities brought to light some interesting differences.   It was found that 34.1 per cent of the white children of native-born fathers were retarded while the retardation among the children of foreign-born fathers was 36 per cent.   Some of the races were notably high in retardation and others were below the average.   The South Italians had 48.6 per cent retarded, the Poles 48.1 per cent, the North Italians 45.9 per cent, while the Finns had only 27.7 per cent retardation.   The Canadians other than French had 27.9 per cent, the Swedes 28.7 per cent, the German Hebrews 29.9 per cent, the Dutch 31.1 per cent, the Welsh 32 per cent, the English 33.7 per cent and the Norwegians 33.9 per cent (70, 354).

The smaller sample of 61,231 pupils, all over eight years old, distributed among twelve cities permits of more detailed analysis (104, 27).   The facts as to retardation are shown in table 15 for the total of 46,836 children who gave data on retardation (104, 31).

Table 15 shows very great differences in the amount of retardation, the smaller percentages being characteristic of the northwestern European stock for the most part.   The very large amount of retardation among the South Italians is in harmony with the findings of Young (145, 20). The question is still open, however, as to the degree to which retardation indicates lack of intelligence. The report shows that retardation is affected by such factors as the birthplace of the pupil, school attendance in other cities, age of the foreign-born pupils at the time of arrival, age of the foreign-born pupils at time of entering school, the ability of the father

TABLE 15

NATIVITY AND RACE OF FATHER	NUMBER GIVING DATA	PER CENT RETARDED
Swedish	1,247	15.5
Canadian (other than French)	1,427	25.8
English	2,086	25.9
Foreign-born English-speaking races	5,295	27.3
Native-born (white)	16,881	28.1
Irish	932	29.0
Scotch	269	32.0
German	4,137	32.8
Bohemian and Moravian	1,282	35.6
Hebrew Russian	5,484	41.8
Foreign-born non-English speaking	23,637	43.4
Portuguese	1,358	45.9
Lithuanian	117	47.9
Canadian French	856	48.1
Italian North	550	51.6
Hebrew Roumanian	241	52.3
Slovak	224	54.5
Italian (not specified)	784	56.1
Magyar	226	58.0
Polish	1,212	58.1
Italian South	2,978	63.6
Hebrew Polish	154	66.9

to speak English, his citizenship, the home language, regularity of school attendance, etc. If these conditions can be shown to produce the differences in amount of retardation, it is impossible to deduce differences in national intelligence from retardation. On the other hand, however, if it be shown that the differences still remain when the various environmental factors are held constant, then it seems probable that the retardation reflects to a certain extent actual lack of capacity. The report gives a table (104, 40) showing the percentage of retardation among the children that were born in the city in which the investigation was made, and hence we have here groups of children from the various nationalities, who are unlikely to have attended school elsewhere than in the city, and whose age and grade of entrance will tend to be the same. The writer worked out a rank order correlation between the percentage retardation for the nationality groups, as given in table 15 and the retardation for these groups when the place of birth was held constant by taking only children who were born in the city where they were studied.[5] Using the Scott Company (122) tables to facilitate the computation, the result was a rho of 0.98. This means that the nationality groups remained in almost exactly the same order when the place of birth was held constant. The equalizing of conditions still left the South Italians with a percentage retardation of 57 per cent as compared with 14 per cent for the Swedish children. It is evident that something more fundamental than place of birth lies back of the original ranking of the nationalities in retardation. There is some relationship between the percentage retardation for the various foreign nationalities as given in table 15, and the percentage of the fathers that do not speak English, as shown by a rho of 0.54 obtained for the 16 nationality groups, for which there is adequate data on the language of the parent (104, 84). Nevertheless, when the language factor is held constant by considering only those children whose fathers spoke English, the correlation of percent retardation with the original ranking in retardation, is 0.94 and we still have a range of from 15 per cent for the Swedes to 59.2 per cent for the South Italians (104, 84). If only those children be considered whose parents have been in this country over twenty years, the order still remains about the same for a correlation of 0.94 is obtained with the original ranking for the 17 groups that are adequately represented (104, 93). The writer next correlated the original figures for retardation as given in table 15 with the percentage retardation in the case of

[5] Since groups were omitted, when so small as to have less than fifty children retarded the coefficient is derived from 18 paired percentages rather than 22. When converted to a Pearson r the coefficient has a probable error of less than 0.02.

children, all of whom came from homes where English was spoken. Taking only the 13 groups that were numerically adequate, a rho of 0.98 was obtained and the differences remained as great as ever. (104, 98). Finally a correlation was worked out for the 22 groups between the percentages of retardation as shown in table 15 and the percentages retarded, when only those children were considered who attended school more than three fourths of the time (104, 110). When the regularity of school attendance was thus made constant, the correlation of percentage retardation with the original figures was 0.96. It is apparent that the original differences and the original rank order of the nationalities in retardation remain in spite of equal environmental conditions, which suggests that real differences in intelligence exist. It should be noted that the environmental handicaps are interrelated, so that holding one factor constant tends to hold the other constant also.

EMINENCE AND NATIONALITY

It is by no means certain that genius is irrepressible (26) but, nevertheless, it is likely that the comparative eminence of the various nationality groups in this country bears some relation to the average capacity of their members. Some slight evidence is available from a study of American men of science but the numbers from particular foreign countries are small and many factors of selection may have affected the immigration of European scientists. The percentage of the men of science studied by Cattell that are foreign-born is only slightly less than the percentage of foreign-born in the population at large. While those born in Great Britain constitute only about 1.2 per cent of the population at large they constitute 3 to 4 per cent of the men of science. The Germans furnish 2.7 per cent of the general population and 1.9 per cent of the scientists, while Italy, contributing 1.5 per cent to the general population, contributes but 0.1 per cent to the men of science (19, 781).

From the point of view of numbers the statistics in Who's Who for 1922–1923 are more satisfactory. Of the total number of names listed, 11.12 per cent or 2430 are names of foreign-born. The writer reduced the data to a common base by referring the number of persons listed as born in a given country to the number of males of that birthplace residing here when the last census was taken in 1920. The results are shown in table 16.

Such data are weak in many ways, from a statistical point of view, since factors of age and sex are not fully controlled, and the average length of residence is not taken into account, but nevertheless, there is a striking contrast between the achievements of the old and the new immigration.[6] As the contribution

TABLE 16

GROUP	NUMBER	NUMBER IN WHO'S WHO PER 100,000 MALES OF THAT NATIVITY IN THE UNITED STATES	RANK
England..........................	445	104.8	1
England, Scotland and Wales......	605	101.5	2
Scotland........................	134	100.0	3
Canada and Newfoundland........	514	92.5	4
France..........................	73	92.0	5
Wales...........................	26	72.1	6
Germany........................	349	50.4	7
Belgium.........................	16	44.5	8
Netherlands.....................	27	35.8	9
Sweden..........................	79	32.9	10
Ireland.........................	142	31.2	11
Denmark........................	31	27.2	12
Scandinavia.....................	155	23.5	13
Norway.........................	45	22.5	14
Austria-Hungary.................	81	15.0	15
Russia..........................	93	12.0	16
Italy...........................	54	5.6	17
Poland..........................	15	2.3	18
Greece..........................	2	1.3	19

of the native-born Americans is 53.5 per 100,000 native-born male whites, it is evident that certain of the foreign nationalities,

[6] The latest volume of Who's Who for 1924–1925 indicates contributions in about the same proportion, save that the absolute numbers of the Polish-born have increased considerably. This would affect the relative position but slightly. The sex factor is not fully controlled for calculation was made by dividing numbers, regardless of sex, by numbers in the male population alone. This causes but a slight error, since less than 10 per cent of the names listed are those of women.

such as the English and Scotch, make contributions that are notably large, in harmony with the earlier findings of Lodge (77). As will be shown later, this evidence will gain in significance by its correspondence with results obtained in other ways.

NATIONAL GROUPS AND FREQUENCY OF MENTAL DEFECT

It is highly desirable to check the results from the application of intelligence tests and other criteria by a study of the relative frequency of mental defect among the different national groups in this country. Unfortunately the data on this subject is comparatively rare, in contrast to data dealing with other types of defect. The most recent study of the subject is a survey carried out for the Committee on Immigration and Naturalization by H. H. Laughlin (2). The method of the survey was to determine the degree to which each nativity group filled its quota for defectiveness, that is to say, the ratio of the proportion of a given group in the institutional population to the proportion of that group in the population at large, as determined from the 1910 census. If the proportions were the same, the quota of 100 per cent would be exactly filled. Of the 657 state or federal institutions in the United States, returns were obtained from 445, of which 32 gave data concerning feeble-mindedness, the only defect which concerns us here.

The results show some interesting contrasts, as for example, the foreign-born white fill their quota only 31.91 per cent P.E. 1.3, while the native whites of native parents have a quota fulfillment of 107.70 P.E. 0.49. For the native whites with one parent native and the other foreign-born, the quota fulfillment is even higher, however, being 190.27 P.E. 2.04. For the native whites with both parents foreign-born it is also high amounting to 165.39 P.E. 1.33. The explanation given by Laughlin for the low quota fulfillment of the foreign-born as compared with the native-born is the effectiveness of the immigration restriction laws which actually keep out the feeble-minded. There are of course other explanations. It is possible that the feeble-minded are not likely to undertake the journey to America, and even more significant is the probability that the foreign-born feeble-minded are not readily detected and rarely find their way to institutions as compared with the native-born. That there is mental defect latent in the foreign stock is clearly shown by the high quota fulfillment for the native-born of foreign-born or mixed parentage.

For many countries the numbers are so small as to yield little information as to the relative tendency of different national groups to mental defect, while in other cases the probable errors are small relative to the percentage quota fulfillment. Great Britain fills its quota to the extent of 27.27, P.E. 4.4, Ireland has but 8.16 P.E. 4.2 and Germany and Scandinavia both fill only about a fifth of their quota. Of the southern and eastern countries, Italy has a quota fulfillment of 25.34 P.E. 4.3, Russia and Finland combined, have 50.53 P.E. 3.7, and Austria-Hungary has 20.99 P.E. 3.8. The figure for Northern Europe is a trifle smaller than for Southern and Eastern Europe, the fulfillment being about 19 as compared with 33, the probable errors being fairly small in both cases (2, 774).

The difficulties in interpretation of facts as to institutional representation by different nationalities are very great and especially so in the matter of mental defect. Since only about 5 per cent of the mental defectives in the United States are in institutions, it is questionable to reason from the proportions who have received institutional care to racial or national characteristics of entire immigrant groups. The fact that the negro who has a marked tendency to mental defect, fills his quota only to the extent of 16.32 P.E. 1.55, at once casts suspicion on the entire procedure.

Gillman has recently made a vigorous attack on Laughlin's entire work, (51) questioning in particular, three premises on which it is based.

I. . . . . That an enumeration of these institutions, and particularly the enumeration as conducted by himself, sufficiently reveals the proportionate occurrence of these inadequacies among the various race and nativity groups.

II. That the data as gathered disclose significant differential occurrences among the various races and nationalities.

III. That the mere occurrence of an inadequacy within a group of individuals of a given race or nativity is a valid proof of the existence of susceptibilities toward the inadequacy as an inborn racial quality . . . . . Dr. Laughlin's fundamental biological assumption (51, 31).

In connection with the first point it is claimed that those groups having a better economic status will take care of their members either in the home or in private institutions. This criticism, while valid to a certain extent, would not explain the low quota fulfillment on the part of the negro. Gillman makes a further criticism that the states included in the sample differed greatly in the proportion of foreign-born in the state populations, and that "as many as sixteen of the twenty-four states lowest in percentage, but only eight of the twenty-four states highest in percentage of foreign-born were omitted in the enumeration of the feeble-minded" (51, 33).

While this criticism is significant still the impression given is not quite correct. Not all of the institutions in the states having a large proportion of foreign-born were included in the sample, in fact, five were omitted in such states as New York, New Jersey and Massachusetts. The omission of these would tend to lower the quota fulfillment of the foreign-born for mental defect.

Furthermore, in many of the states which Gillman refers to as having been omitted there were no institutions at all for the feeble-minded. Of the 17 institutions that were omitted 10 were in states having a high proportion of foreign-born. While the selection by institutions is favorable rather than unfavorable to the showing of the foreign-born, the reverse is true, as Gillman points out, when the selection by states is considered.

The use of the probable error method by Laughlin is criticized with some justice. The method will correct or control the matter of numbers only and not errors in sampling. Very large probable errors were often neglected after having been calculated. Gillman criticizes further the use of the 1910 census figures, the ignoring of sex and age factors, and the interpretation of the facts. His claim, however, that traits are not hereditary when they fail to correlate one with another, is not in the least convincing.

In conclusion it may be admitted that Laughlin's data are open to criticism on many points and that it is extremely doubtful whether relative tendencies to mental defect between immigrant groups can be determined by an analysis of the institutional population. At most there is a suggestion that the immigrants themselves, especially those from Northern Europe, compare very favorably with the native-born in freedom from mental defect, but that considerable feeble-mindedness is latent in the stock.

MENTAL DEFECTIVES IN THE ARMY

Far more accurate than any institutional statistics of mental defect are the Army data. If the draft is at all a fair cross section of the population at large, then the cases of mental defect brought to light in the camps are likely to be in proportions that fairly represent the proportions in the country at large. According to Bailey, of the 72,323 cases of nervous and mental disorders identified by the Medical Corps examiners in the United States, 22,741 or 31.4 per cent were mental defectives. "If the mental defectives rejected at the local boards are added to those rejected at the camps, the total number of individuals seriously handicapped by mental defect brought to light by the mobilization reaches 26,545" (7, 1). In addition, there were the 1475 cases found in France and those found at the demobilization examination. Furthermore some were doubtless discharged under a different diagnosis, and some doubtless settled down to a certain degree of usefulness in menial occupations in the army. The value of this data as confirmatory evidence lies in the fact that the defectives were detected for the most part by their poor adaptation to army conditions and independently of mental tests. About 42 per cent were detected by psychiatrists in routine examinations, about 28 per cent by other medical officers, about 26 per cent by commanding officers and about 4 per cent by psychologists. The small number of defectives detected by psychologists was chiefly due to the administrative situation whereby they had little or no power of recommendation. Of the 21,858 studied, 81.5 per cent were discharged and others may have been discharged on a second recommendation. This indicates that in most of the cases the inadequacy was very real, and hardly to be attributed to mere environmental circumstances.

The classification of the defectives by nativity unfortunately only gives the absolute numbers and not the proportion referred to the totals of the different nativity groups in the army. In the case of about a hundred thousand soldiers, taken for an analysis of test results, the numbers of foreign-born were such as to indicate that the proportion in the army corresponded fairly closely to the proportion in the population at large.   Therefore the best that can be done is to divide the number of defectives of a given nativity by the number of males of that nativity in the country at large between the ages of 20 and 44, thus obtaining a basis for a comparison of relative frequency of mental defect. On this basis the writer found that of the native-born whites including those of foreign and mixed parentage 110.9 per 100,000 enter the army and are classified as mental defectives.   For the native colored, the corresponding figure is 213, and for the foreign-born white 51.5.   In the case of the latter it is of course possible that fewer entered the army because of non-citizenship, and thus lowered the proportion of defectives, but the draft requirements were such that it is unlikely that the proportion of foreign-born exempted was much greater than for the native-born.   In general these figures must be regarded as more significant than those based on the proportions of different nationalities or nativity groups in institutions, and yet confirming the results of Laughlin's study indicating a slighter tendency to mental defect among the foreign-born than among the native-born.

Considering the foreign-born only, there are notable differences in the tendency to feeble-mindedness between the various racial and national groups.   There are two ways in which the tendency to mental defect may be determined.   One is to divide the absolute numbers of defectives born in a given country by the number of hundred thousand males of that nativity in the United States. This is of course based on the assumption that the proportion of a given nativity in the army represents the proportion of that nativity in the population at large.   Another index of the relative strength of the tendency to mental defect is the percent of the total neuropsychiatric cases of a given nativity or race who are feeble-minded.   For example of the total number of neuropsychiatric cases listed by Bailey (7, 28) as of the Mexican race, 257 or 66.9 per cent were diagnosed as feeble-minded.   In table 17 the relative tendency to mental defect of immigrants born in various countries, as determined by both methods, is presented. It is apparent that there is a rough correspondence between the rankings according to the two methods, in fact, a rank order coefficient of correlation amounts to 0.72.

If the classification be made by race, rather than country of birth, there are marked differences in the percentage of the total neuropsychiatric cases of each race that are feeble-minded. There are 66.9 per cent feeble-minded among the neuropsychiatric cases listed as being of the Mexican race, and 62.9 per cent in the case of the American Indian, followed in order by the Armenian, the Slavonic, Italian, English, French, Spanish, German, Dutch, Greek, Scandinavian, Irish, Hebrew, Welsh and Scotch (7, 28–29).

TABLE 17

COUNTRY OF BIRTH	NUMBER F.M. SOLDIERS	NUMBER PER 100,000 MALES IN UNITED STATES OF THAT NATIVITY	RANK	PER CENT F.M. OF TOTAL NEUROPSYCHIATRIC CASES OF THAT NATIVITY	RANK
Russia	538	69.6	1	32.1	3
Italy	663	69.4	2	32.5	2
Greece	58	40.4	3	24.0	8
Netherlands	22	29.2	4	25.6	6
Poland	144	22.3	5	43.5	1
Austria-Hungary	154	17.9	6	31.1	4
Ireland	59	12.95	7	28.4	5
Canada	72	12.91	8	21.4	9
Scandinavia	85	12.8	9	18.8	11
France	10	12.6	10	20.4	10
Germany	48	5.4	11	25.7	7
England, Scotland and Wales.	30	5.0	12	9.2	12

Rho = 0.72.

The results show rather clearly a tendency to mental defect somewhat stronger for the newer immigrant stock from southern and eastern Europe, although there are several marked exceptions. This tendency is somewhat more definite than that shown by Laughlin's data. A rank order correlation between the number of feeble-minded in the Army for each 100,000 of the male population born in a given foreign country and his results, in the case of ten countries for which there is comparable data, shows a coefficient of only about 0.30. It is likely that the study of the problem, by the use of data from institutional populations, is bound to give an inaccurate picture of the relative tendency to defect in various groups which are not uniformly affected by forces making for institutional segregation.

TABLE 18

Rank order in mentality according to investigations described

GROUP	I	II	III	IV	V	VI	VII	VIII	IX	X	XI	XII	XIII
American			1	2	3	1	1	2	1	2			
English	1	4			1			1			3	1	
Scotland	2											3	
England, Scotland and Wales				1								2	1
Great Britain										3			
Holland	3											8	9
Canada	4			3	2						2	4	5
Germany	5	2			4			3		5	6	7	2
Denmark	6									10		11	
Sweden	7	3								4	1	9	
Danish and Swedish				5									
Norway	8	1								9		13	
Scandinavia												12	4
Ireland	9			7							4	10	6
French		6		6								5	3
Canadian French											11		
Bohemian and Moravian											7		
Lithuanian											10		
Austria	10	5											
Hungary					5			4					
Austria-Hungary											7	14	7
Jewish			2	4									
Hebrew Roumanian											1	13	
Hebrew Russian											6	8	
Hebrew Polish												17	
Finnish		7								8			
Slovak		8										14	
Slavish								6					
Russian	11				6							15	12
Poland	14			8	7					11	15	17	8
Greece	12											18	10
Italy	13	9	4	9	8	2	2	7	2	12		16	11
Italian North												12	
Italian South												16	
Mexican					3								
Portuguese					4						9		
Colored			3	10				5	3				

TABLE 18—*Continued*

Correlations for corresponding groups

I and XII... rho 0.94
I and XI.. rho 0.55
I and XIII.. rho 0.68
XI and XIII... rho 0.78

   I. Army Test, Per Cent A and B.
   II. Brown S-B Tests.
   III. Murdock.
   IV. Feingold (3 classes combined).
   V. Detroit Tests, Per Cent Group X.
   VI. Young.
   VII. Dickson.
   VIII. Pintner.
   IX. Arlitt.
   X. Jordan.
   XI. Immig. Com. Retardation Data.
   XII. Who's Who.
   XIII. F. M. Soldiers.

AGREEMENT IN RESULTS

The problem of mental differences between immigrant groups has been approached from various angles. The next step is to consider the degree to which the results correspond in pointing to a definite conclusion. This can be done by bringing together the rankings of the immigrant groups as determined by the various studies that deal with any considerable number of groups, and then correlating the results. This has been done in table 18.

CONCLUSION

Table 18 shows that the various investigations tend to an agreement in results. The small number of cases in certain investigations make the correlation less striking than might otherwise have been the case. It is especially interesting to note that where the samples are adequate in size there is a correspondence between the results of mental tests and the frequency of mental defect. Since the latter is principally due to heredity it suggests that achievement on mental tests is also largely determined by heredity. Bearing in mind the other studies, covering but a few groups and not listed in the summary table, the conclusion seems to be that in general the representatives of the newer immigration, especially the Latins, have less intelligence than the Americans or those of the older immigrant stock. This is but a tentative conclusion, however, that must stand or fall with further evidence, and it is very probable that the groups of lower intelligence are considerably handicapped by unfavorable environmental conditions. One aim of the detailed study to be presented in the next chapter is to investigate the influence of linguistic factors on test achievement.

CHAPTER III

The Detailed Research

A detailed study was made in Massachusetts of children of certain immigrant groups, with two objects in mind, first, to determine the average intelligence of the groups as compared with each other and with American children, in order to evaluate the effect of these streams of immigration upon the general level of intelligence, and second, to determine the significance of an unfavorable linguistic background upon test achievement. The groups studied were French Canadians, Finns, Italians, and Americans. The study was begun in January, 1923, and data were collected over a period of several months. These immigrant groups are among the most important from the point of view of numbers in the particular section of New England in which it was convenient to make the study, and the French Canadians and Italians make up a considerable percentage of the foreign born population, taken the country over. The latter, in a sense, are typical of the "New Immigration" from southern Europe.

ANTHROPOLOGICAL AND SOCIOLOGICAL BACKGROUNDS

A word should be said concerning the racial and sociological characteristics of the immigrant groups studied. The concept of race is vague at the present time and certainly most peoples are racially very much mixed (55, 128) so that racial interpretations are uncertain. There is no intention of extending the implications of this study to races as a whole. The French Canadians illustrate the difficulties in the way of identifying a locality, linguistic, or cultural group with a distinct race. Alpine, Nordic, and perhaps Mediterranean types, were doubtless well mixed before the movement of colonists from the west coast of France to the New World began in the seventeenth century. If any conclusion at all can be ventured, it would be to the effect that the predominant type was Alpine. For the most part the colonists were of a sturdy peasant stock (79). The immigration to the United States began as early as 1834 and, according to Belcourt (8), a total of some 1,750,000 have come to the United States, most of them from Quebec. The increase was most rapid from 1880 to 1890 when they came in great numbers to enter the shoe factories and the textile mills (69). Since 1910 there has been some decline but still, according to the 1920 census figures, 307,786 or 2.2 per cent of the entire foreign-born population, were listed as French Canadians born in Canada, of which Massachusetts has 108,681 (Vol. 11, p. 698).

By 1885 there were considerable numbers of French Canadians in Fitchburg (33, 554), Leominster (33, 556), and Northbridge (33, 557), the three towns where children were tested. The movement took place a trifle earlier in the case of the latter town, and the proportion of French Canadians in the population has been larger, but in general the conditions are much the same. Fitchburg and Leominster have at the present time about the same proportion of French Canadians, and in both there is a certain amount of concentration of these people in a single district. The economic status is similar, perhaps a trifle better in the latter city. In the ward of Fitchburg in which the French Canadians are concentrated in greatest numbers, the number of persons per room is 1, while for the entire city it is only 0.8 (31, p. 89). Dexter has discussed the sociological traits of the French Canadian, such as intense group consciousness and religious conservatism (36).

Little need be said concerning the Italians. They probably are predominantly of Mediterranean stock with some admixture of Alpine, possibly a little Saracen blood and traces of an ancient negroid strain (145, 74–75), (62).

The motive for immigration is even more distinctly economic (42, 104) than in the case of the French Canadians. During the first decade of the twentieth century there was a flood of Italian immigration amounting to one or two hundred thousand a year. The movement is considerably more recent than that of the French Canadians, for in 1885 there were but 7 Italians in Fitchburg out of a foreign-born population of 3687 (33, 554) and an equally insignificant number in Leominster. At the present time the Italian-born comprise about 2.5 per cent of the total population in Fitchburg and about 5 per cent in Leominster. In both cities there is considerable concentration in distinct districts and in both cases most of the Italian children of the entire city are to be found in a single school.

The anthropology of the Finns has long been a source of controversy (102), (65), a settlement of which need not be attempted here. Confusion of language and race has caused the Finns to be identified racially with the Magyars and in the popular mind they are not clearly distinguished from the Lapps. Peake (91) has taken up the problem and claims that the Finns are both Nordic and Asiatic in type but that their language is of Asiatic derivation. Ripley inclines to consider them fundamentally Nordic (105, 359–364). Dominian tends to agree with Peake (quoted 132). In spite of the scanty resources in Finland a rather high civilization has been built up. The school system is complete and efficient and for a long time literacy has been very high. From 1899–1909, only 1.4 per cent of the Finnish immigrant over 14 were illiterate (70, 35). Perhaps there is a certain eugenic significance in the attitude of the clergy who in many cases refuse to marry illiterates. While Finnish immigration has had economic motives, there seems evidence that the desire for freedom and resentment at the Russian attempt to reduce Finland to her direct control had some effect.

A few Finns came as early as the middle of the last century, settling the Lake Superior district. Following 1885, settlement began in Lanesville, Mass. (4). Following 1900, several thousand came each year to the United States, so that, while in 1900 there were 62,641 Finnish-born, by 1920, there were 149,824, of which 14,570 are in Massachusetts. According to the Massachusetts Census of 1885, there were no Finns listed and very few Russians, who might have been Finns, in either Fitchburg (33, 554), or in Maynard, the two towns in which Finnish children were studied. In 1895 there were 483 persons in Fitchburg who were born in Russia out of a total population of 26,409 (32, 678) and in Maynard there were 115 out of 3090 (32, 643). Ten years later Finns were listed, as such, and amounted to about 6 per cent of the entire population in Fitchburg and about 19 per cent of the population in Maynard. Since this time there has been little increase in Maynard, while in Fitchburg there has been an increase of about 50 per cent. In general the Finnish immigration must be considered to have taken place after the French Canadian and at about the same time as the Italian, although attaining considerable proportions a little earlier. In Fitchburg the concentration of the Finns in a single locality is not so marked as in the case of the French Canadians. There are really two centers of Finnish residence in wards 1 and 4 and the children were to be found in large numbers in two schools, both of which were visited for testing purposes. In Ward 1 the number of persons to a room is 0.8, the same as for the entire city, and in Ward 4, it is 0.6, so that if these figures are any index the Finns seem to live in a "good neighborhood" and to resemble their American neighbors in standard of living (31, 89).

THE TESTS USED

The tests used were the Illinois Examination (83) and the Army Beta Test, one being rather verbal in type and the other rather strictly a performance test. The Illinois Examination contains a reading and an arithmetic test as well as an intelligence test and, therefore, achievement quotients may be calculated. It was hoped that a comparison of the results of the verbal and the nonverbal tests would give an insight into the influence of the language factor, and that the reading test would give still further information.

The Illinois Examination is highly objective both in administration and in correcting. Its reliability is shown by the fact that two forms of the intelligence test were found to correlate to an extent of 0.92 P.E. 0.006. The probable error of estimate from a true score is only 5.3, which means that on the intelligence tests one-half of the cases will be in error less than 5.3 points, which is about 10 per cent of the average score made. This amount of error is not insignificant but it is no greater than that of standard individual tests, being about the same as for the Stanford-Binet. Such an inaccuracy would have little affect on group comparisons. The Illinois Test correlates highly with the Stanford-Binet, the National Intelligence Test, and the Otis Group Test (83). Root obtained correlations somewhat smaller (106).

The Beta test was designed for the use of illiterates and the foreign-born in the army. While intended for adults, rather than for children, it is one of the best performance tests and its previous use makes possible certain valuable comparisons. The Beta tests show a fair correlation with Stanford-Binet ratings. A correlation was derived from a sample of 653 cases taken from several camps, using raw Beta scores which were ultimately adopted, since weighting did not raise the correlation. This correlation was 0.737 P.E. 0.012 (81, 390) which is as large as the correlation of the verbal Illinois test with the Stanford-Binet. The correlation of Beta with Alpha, a test of proven worth, is high, 0.811 P.E. 0.009, when raw scores are used. This is slightly raised by using a correlation ratio in order to take into account the curvilinear relationship (81, 392).

OTHER DATA

In addition to test material, a certain amount of data was obtained regarding teacher's estimates of intelligence, grade location and school marks. The estimates were made by the teachers using a scale ranging from one to seven and the marks were the average obtained in all subjects over a period of several months. A special investigation in Fitchburg high school resulted in some valuable information chiefly in connection with the academic achievement of the Finns. A questionnaire was used in the grammar schools in addition to the questions as to age, grade, school, etc., that were asked on the examination blanks. The accuracy of the replies obviously depended in part on the intelligence of the child and, as was to be expected, the data were not complete in every case. Some of the questions check each other, and additional information was obtained from teachers in regard to age, so that errors in this respect, if any, are slight. Fairly satisfactory data was obtained concerning social backgrounds of each child, as to place of birth of self, father, mother and, in many cases of grandparents; occupation of father, language spoken with each parent, number of years in school, number of rooms in home, number of persons occupying them, etc.

THE SAMPLES

The children studied were all eleven years of age, although in some cases it was impossible to find a room where the children of the wrong age could be sent, whereupon they would also be tested but the results discarded. By keeping the age factor constant it is possible to make comparisons of groups without resort to the use of the I.Q. The children were classified as being of a given nationality only when both of the parents were of that nationality. In general the number of mixed marriages was surprisingly few. The nationality of the parents was determined by country of birth, save in the case of French Canadians when name and language both marked them clearly as of that stock, even though born in this country. A very few children, whose parents were born in either England or Scotland, were classified as Americans but beyond this no exceptions were made. The rigid system of classification isolated a certain number of cases of children who were of the wrong age, of mixed marriages, or of other nationalities, but this data has been excluded from the study save for incidental reference.

The sample of Finns was taken from four schools, two in Fitchburg and two in Maynard, together with about a half dozen from miscellaneous schools. In every case, however, the children were from the public schools. The Fitchburg schools will be referred to as the AH and the L schools and those in Maynard as the R and the B schools.

French Canadian children were studied in the parochial schools A of Leominster, the parochial school B of Fitchburg and the public school C in Northbridge. The Italian children were for the most part from the L public school in Leominster and the N public school in Fitchburg, together with miscellaneous cases from other public schools. The Americans were found in all of the public schools studied, but in no one place in sufficient number to be considered separately. Great care was taken in every case to test all of the children that were eleven years old in every school, regardless of grade. In a few cases children were absent, but rarely did they miss both tests and there is no reason to think that there was any selective influence through absences.

Very few of the total number of children tested had had any experience with mental tests and none had had the particular tests used. Since there was no notice given of the tests to be used, there was no opportunity for coaching and this would have been very unlikely in any case.

METHODS OF GIVING TESTS

The tests were all given by the writer and for the most part under fairly satisfactory conditions. In most cases the tests were given in the morning, but in a few cases at the opening of the school in the afternoon. The numbers tested at one time were never over fifty, in most cases about half that number, and every effort was made to keep the subtle psychological conditions of morale, attention, and incentive, as constant as possible. The A group of French Canadian children showed more intense interest than those from the B or the N schools. The conditions in the B school will be discussed later. The Italians of the N school were eager, while those of the L school were less responsive. In all of the other schools there was uniform interest and cooperation. It is very hard to separate the factors of interest and alertness from intelligence proper for an intelligent group of children are stimulated by their own success. In giving the Illinois tests the handbook was followed exactly with the sole exception that the directions were repeated if there was any sign of lack of comprehension. It was felt that accuracy would be furthered by insuring an understanding of the test requirements, even if repetitions were quite unnecessary for the brighter pupils. The verbal directions used with the Beta tests were the same as those used by Young. Diagrams were drawn with india ink on large pieces of cardboard corresponding exactly to the demonstration charts used in the army procedure (81, p. 164, Plates 15 and 16). Care was taken that the demonstration should be clearly visible to all of the pupils and the pantomine was repeated if any sign of incomprehension followed the request that any child who failed to understand should raise his hand. The correcting was done by the writer and one assistant with the aid of celluloid stencils. The rechecking of a considerable number of tests showed no mistakes.

RESULTS FROM TEACHERS ESTIMATES OF INTELLIGENCE
AND FROM MARKS

The teachers estimates of intelligence were not of the value that was hoped for, in view of the fact that a set of ratings could not be carried over and compared to the ratings from another school because of the difference in school standards. The ratings can only be considered of real significance when they apply to pupils in the same school, and unfortunately the pupils of a single school tended to be predominantly of one nationality. However, a small number of Italians and Americans attended the same schools and their standing may be compared according to a teachers rating of intelligence. The difference in standing is marked. Of the 22 Americans about 9 per cent were in class 2, i.e., considered of superior intelligence, while only about 5 per cent of the 38 Italians were given this rating. In class 3 the Americans had 41 per cent, while the Italians had 52 per cent as compared with 41 per cent for the Americans, and continued to have a larger percentage receiving the lower ratings. There were 5 per cent who received a rating of 7, which was not given to any of the Americans. This crumb of evidence points clearly to inferiority of Italian children according to the judgments of teachers. The same results are shown by a comparison of the averaged school marks for the same groups. For each individual the marks in various subjects were averaged, and the mean of these averaged marks was computed for the group. The mean of the marks of the Americans was 80.6 as compared with 71.81 for the Italians.

In the case of the Finns and Americans the differences are not so marked, but the Finns are at least equal, if not superior, according to teachers ratings, of intelligence. Of 31 Americans, 6.4 per cent are rated 2, while of 49 Finns in the same school, 4.1 per cent are given this rating. But in class 3, which is above the average on a scale of 7, the Finns have 34.6 per cent as compared with 19.5 per cent for the Americans. The distribution at the lower levels was about the same for both groups. The Americans tended to the average, with 67.8 per cent as compared with 43 per cent receiving a rating of 4. The results of a comparison of marks are much the same. Thirty Americans have 80.6 as the mean of their school marks while 52 Finns in the same school have a mean of 82.2 per cent.

These facts may be supplemented to a certain extent by the results of an investigation of Finnish achievement in the Fitchburg High School, which was chiefly concerned with marks and honors. There is a marked tendency for the Finns to take advantage of educational opportunities, and in 1923 there were 22 Finns in a senior class of 198, or a little over 11 per cent. Of the 22, there were 8 who attained honors.[1]

Of the fifty pupils in the Junior class in 1922–1923 obtaining honors, 14, or about 28 per cent were Finns. In the Sophomore class of the same year, of the 51 receiving honors, 18, or about 35 per cent were Finns. In the Freshman class there were 17 Finns, out of the 66 who received honors. It was not possible to determine the proportion of Finns in these lower classes taken as a whole, but it is certain that it was much lower than the proportion among the honor students.

Even more exact data is available from the records for January and February, 1924. Among the Seniors, the Finns numbered 30, in a class which had an average enrollment for the year of 224, that is to say, they comprised 13.4 per cent of the class and yet furnished 9, or 19.5 per cent, of the 46 honor students. Of the Junior class, which had an average enrollment of 241, 41 or about 17 per cent, were Finns and yet of the 50 receiving honor marks for the two-month period, 16, or about 32 per cent were of this nationality. The proportion of Finns in the Sophomore class could not be determined but they contributed 12 out of the 40

[1] A certain amount of evidence from mental tests was also available. Terman group tests had been given to all of the freshmen of 1922–1923 and after identification of nationality by the Principal, it was possible to compare the scores of 26 Finns with those of 83 non-Finns, mostly Americans of the higher social classes. The median I.Q. for the non-Finnish group was 97.10, while that for the Finns was 94. The seniors of the high school were tested in 1922 in connection with the Massachusetts Mental Survey and in this case 19 Finns out of a total of 167 tested attained a median score of 44.9 on the Brown University Test as compared with 42.5 for the entire group taken as a whole. In test achievement, Finnish pupils seem to be about equal to the other high school pupils.

honor students, or 30 per cent. Consistent with these facts is the distribution of gold letters, given for two successive years of high scholarship, for of the 18 pupils winning the gold letters, 4, or 22.2 per cent were Finns. The conclusion would seem to be that the Finnish pupils in the high school are equal if not superior to the other nationalities in intelligence.

RESULTS AS TO GRADE LOCATION

Returning to the grammar school data we find that here the facts concerning grade location are more valuable than data concerning school marks and intelligence ratings. It is still a

TABLE 19

Percentage grade distribution and mean grade location

GROUP	NUMBER OF CASES	PER CENT FIRST GRADE	PER CENT SECOND GRADE	PER CENT THIRD GRADE	PER CENT FOURTH GRADE	PER CENT FIFTH GRADE	PER CENT SIXTH GRADE	PER CENT SEVENTH GRADE	MEAN GRADE LOCATION
Americans..................	97	0	0	0	8.25	39.2	52.5	0	5.94
Finns......................	145	0	0	2.36	11.7	43.5	42.7	0	5.77
Italians....................	100	0	2.0	13.0	48.0	17.0	16.0	4.0	4.84
F, C.......................	176	0	0.58	9.67	21.6	38.6	21.6	8.0	5.56
A, F, C....................	54	0	0	0	12.9	35.0	42.5	9.26	5.98
B, F, C....................	85	0	0	18.5	29.5	36.4	7.1	10.6	5.16
C and Miscellaneous........	36	0	2.7	8.10	16.2	48.5	24.4	0	5.28

question, however, whether a given grade location in a parochial school has exactly the same significance as a similar grade location in a public school, for certainly the criteria on which the location is made, differ considerably. Still the data shown in table 19 must be considered of considerable significance and, as will be shown later, there is a high correlation between the scores on the tests and grade location. Table 19 gives the percentage in the various grades and the mean grade location, thus showing the range and variability, as well as the central tendency. The mean for the Americans is the highest, but exceeds the Finns by an amount so small as to have little significance. The range of distribution is very short, but this is largely due to the fact that in one school, from which many of the American children came, the Principal objected to very marked advancement on the grounds of possible social maladjustment. A comparison with the Finns is quite fair, for the Americans and Finns were largely from the same schools. The range and variability of the Finns is slight for the same reason as in the case of the Americans, and the central tendency is slightly lower, but the difference is so small as to have no significance. The Italians were all from the public schools and their inferiority, as shown by grade location, is quite significant, amounting, as it does, to an average divergence of over a grade, from both the Finnish and American means. In the case of the French Canadians the range is much greater, due merely to a different school policy in the parochial schools. Under that same policy, no doubt many of the Finns and Americans would be in the seventh grade, and the central tendency raised accordingly. Even with the children in the higher grades, the French Canadians, taken as a whole, have a lower central tendency than do the Americans and Finns. The considerable difference between the two parochial schools is significant in view of the great differences in test results for the two places.

THE TEST RESULTS, BY SCHOOLS

Before considering the results when the different national groups are taken as units, which are set forth below in table 21, it is well to consider the results by schools. This will give insight into the degree to which the racial groups are homogeneous in achievement, in spite of attending different schools and living in different localities. Such a brief, detailed consideration will prevent the swallowing up and obscuring of certain significant facts by massed grouping. It must be remembered, however, that the numbers of a given racial group in a particular school, are often so small as to merit little attention, or permit little detailed treatment. In table 20 the means of the various sub-groups are given, and in some cases, also the medians, when another measure of central tendency seemed justified. In the case of the Americans, it is evident that wherever there is a sample of reasonable size from a school, there is a uniformly, high mean score on both Illinois and Beta. Since the Americans represent three different schools and two different towns, it is evident that we are dealing with a homogeneous sample. While only about a hundred cases of Americans were obtained, they seem quite representative of such children in Massachusetts.[2]

TABLE 20

Means of test scores by schools

GROUP	NUMBER OF CASES	MEAN ILLINOIS SCORES	NUMBER OF CASES	MEAN BETA SCORES
Americans:				
H School, Fitchburg............	15	84.20	15	72.53
HA School, Fitchburg..........	33	63.18	34	64.16
R School, Maynard.............	21	73.95	21	68.09
L School, Leominster...........	9	48.33	9	58.83
Miscellaneous schools..........	16	61.75	16	64.06
Finns:				
R and B Schools, Maynard......	50	58.32	52	63.55
HA School, Fitchburg..........	57	57.50	54	64.53
L School, Fitchburg............	37	61.16	34	64.74
Italians:				
L School, Leominster...........	30	38.63	31	51.39
N School, Fitchburg............	45	47.70	45	55.30
H School, Fitchburg............	8	39.20	7	52.50
R School, Maynard.............	6	26.80	6	53.90
Miscellaneous schools..........	7	31.70	6	50.20
French Canadians:				
A School, Leominster..........	53	58.24	47	60.43
B School, Fitchburg............	73	31.76	77	45.79
C School, Northbridge..........	29	44.72	31	51.51
Miscellaneous Northern Europeans:				
Lithuanian, German, Swede, Danish......................	24	61.25	25	65.70
Miscellaneous Southern and Eastern Europeans:				
Jew, Greek, Pole...............	27	57.68	27	62.50

Homogeneity of the sample is also clearly indicated in the case of the Finns. The representatives of the different schools and

[2] A group of 25, unselected, eleven-year-old American children, from another school, tested with the Illinois test by E. A. Kirkpatrick, were found to have a median mental score of 66.5, which is in very close agreement, and leads to the general conclusion, that a larger number of American children would not have greatly changed the results.

localities show an achievement on both the Illinois and the Beta tests that remains very nearly constant. The Italians uniformly stand on a lower level of achievement than the Americans and Finns, but the means of the school group are quite similar, whenever the group is of sufficient size to avoid chance fluctuations. The constancy of achievement is especially apparent in the case of the means of the Beta scores. There is some slight indication that the Fitchburg Italians are superior to those from Leominster.

Examination of the table shows that, in the case of the French Canadians, it is a different story, for the children from the A school stand very much higher on both tests than do the children from the B school. It is apparent that very real differences exist in the character of the two school populations, which may be due to either innate or acquired traits. That this is a result of the size of the samples is not likely, for the groups are of considerable size.

Furthermore, data is available for an additional 38 children from the A school, who were under the age desired, all being ten years old. These ten-year-old children were found to have a median score of 50 on the Illinois test, and 53.25 on the Beta tests, which corresponds to the achievement of the A eleven-year-olds, the difference in age being taken into account. In fact the A ten-year-olds stand above the B eleven-year-olds on both tests and even exceed a small group of 23 Fitchburg twelve-year-olds. It is evident, therefore, that the sub-samples of French Canadians should be considered separately, which has been done in the pages following.[3]

The small group of miscellaneous North Europeans consists of Lithuanians, Germans, Swedes and Danes, these being combined with Americans and Finns to give the large group of North Europeans of table 21. This classification is made to test the alleged superiority of the "Nordic" North European. The group of

[3] That the French Canadian pupils of the C school really are no higher in intelligence than is indicated by the sample of the eleven-year-olds is shown by the fact that the median I.Q. for the 25 pupils, excluded from the tabulation, because over age, is only 85.83. This median I.Q. is even lower than the I.Q. of, roughly, 91, that would correspond to the mean score of 44.72, for the eleven-year-old children, as given in table 20.

TABLE 21

Measures of central tendency, of dispersion and percentiles of major groups

GROUP	NUMBER	M	σ_m	$P.E._m$	Mdn	σ_{Mdn}	P.E. Mdn	σ_{Dist}	σ_c	$P.E._\sigma$	q	P_5	P_{10}	P_{20}	P_{25}	P_{30}	P_{40}	P_{50}	P_{60}	P_{70}	P_{75}	P_{80}	P_{90}	P_{95}
								Illinois Scores																
Americans	94	67.17	2.15	1.44	67.50	2.69	1.84	21.10	1.37	0.92	13.76	32.70	40.33	49.75	54.50	57.10	62.25	67.50	72.70	78.43	82.08	85.66	98.0	103.25
Finns	147	58.42	1.69	1.14	57.83	2.27	1.42	20.17	1.18	0.79	12.55	27.27	33.56	40.40	46.39	47.96	52.78	57.83	63.72	68.72	71.50	75.00	87.95	94.37
B, French Canadians	73	31.76	1.95	1.31	28.54	2.67	1.64	16.65	1.38	0.93	10.57	10.40	12.70	18.00	20.58	22.23	25.50	28.54	33.17	39.25	41.72	44.00	52.83	60.75
A, French Canadians	53	58.24	2.25	1.51	57.50	4.20	1.90	16.35	1.59	1.07	15.50	34.15	36.92	41.00	42.63	44.68	51.20	57.50	63.80	71.94	73.63	75.00	79.75	84.17
All French Canadians	158	43.31	1.60	1.08	41.47	1.96	1.32	20.10	1.13	0.76	14.38	12.45	17.33	25.19	27.68	30.22	37.00	41.47	46.52	54.74	56.44	61.50	74.0	79.28
Italians	96	41.21	2.09	1.41	39.28	2.26	1.66	19.30	1.39	0.94	14.23	15.80	20.72	24.63	26.54	28.36	33.00	39.28	45.73	50.20	55.00	59.80	69.40	78.25
Northern Europeans	265	62.20	1.28	0.88	59.32	1.77	1.08	20.90	0.91	0.61	14.10	30.78	31.72	43.84	48.33	50.57	56.15	59.32	67.41	72.86	76.53	81.15	88.40	97.08
Southern and Eastern Europeans	123	45.38	1.82	1.23	43.25	2.60	1.54	20.16	1.28	0.86	15.42	17.15	21.38	26.38	28.74	31.45	37.60	43.25	48.66	56.16	59.58	64.37	71.70	79.75
								Beta Scores																
Americans	95	65.83	1.21	0.815	66.25	1.66	1.02	11.80	0.86	0.58	7.81	46.25	49.64	55.91	58.06	60.17	63.33	66.25	68.90	71.97	73.68	75.55	81.50	87.00
Finns	141	64.19	0.99	0.67	66.19	1.53	0.83	11.80	0.70	0.47	8.53	45.21	47.95	53.00	56.43	58.76	62.60	66.19	69.04	72.01	73.50	74.96	81.22	83.37
B, French Canadians	77	45.79	1.59	1.07	44.77	2.34	1.34	13.95	1.13	0.76	10.58	19.75	29.63	34.62	36.35	37.96	41.73	44.77	51.83	56.30	57.52	58.86	63.58	68.49
A, French Canadians	47	60.43	1.32	0.89	59.64	2.57	1.12	10.96	1.13	0.76	8.39	45.85	47.32	50.25	51.72	53.19	56.28	59.64	63.00	66.58	68.50	70.60	75.50	79.50
All French Canadians	158	51.43	1.18	0.789	53.16	1.52	1.00	14.87	0.836	0.56	10.34	27.90	32.41	38.42	41.25	44.07	48.88	53.16	56.69	59.73	61.94	64.50	70.75	76.43
Italians	95	53.41	1.56	1.05	52.50	1.82	1.32	15.21	1.10	0.74	9.42	28.75	32.75	42.00	43.90	45.10	49.25	52.50	56.00	60.20	62.75	65.50	75.20	80.40
Northern Europeans	260	65.32	0.74	0.50	66.06	0.05	0.62	11.90	0.523	0.352	8.14	45.53	48.94	55.00	57.40	59.83	63.05	66.06	68.82	71.94	73.68	75.45	81.30	84.13
Southern and Eastern Europeans	122	55.49	1.31	0.885	54.76	1.56	0.92	14.50	0.73	0.626	8.95	28.89	37.75	44.00	46.09	48.00	51.52	54.76	58.11	62.25	65.00	67.54	76.29	84.50

miscellaneous South and East Europeans consists of Jews (Polish), Poles and Greeks. Together with the Italians, they go to make up the group of South and East Europeans of table 21. These miscellaneous groups, compared with each other, show a slight superiority of the North Europeans on both tests, but rather because they are above average, than because the Southern Europeans are below the average. The latter scores almost fifty-seven points on the Illinois test, which corresponds to a mental age of between eleven years and eleven years, six months, or, but little below that which would be expected for a group of eleven-year-olds.[4]

GENERAL RESULTS AS TO COMPARATIVE CENTRAL TENDENCIES

Taking the national groups as a unit, in so far as they are homogeneous, it is now possible to compare in detail the central tendencies of these larger groups. The results are presented in table 21 which gives means and medians and measures of their reliability (111, 228–232), (74, 90).

A mere glance at the main table shows clearly that there are two levels of achievement on the Illinois test. On the upper level we find the Americans with the Finns somewhat below. On the lower level of achievement we find the French Canadians taken as a whole, with the Italians a trifle below. If the French Canadians, however, be divided into groups A and B, the former group approaches the upper level, and the latter lies below the Italians on the lower level. In the case of the Beta scores, the same general order is maintained, but the differences are notably reduced. On the upper level the Americans and Finns show almost the same achievement, and on the lower level the French Canadians taken as a group and the Italians are almost equal. As in the case of the Illinois scores, if the French Canadian groups be divided, the sub-groups A and B stand respectively above and below the Italians.

[4] It is perhaps worthy of mention that a group of 23 Polish children of various ages but averaging about 11 had a median I.Q. of 100.62. This is interesting, in view of the poor showing of the Polish adults on the army tests (81, 697). There is some suggestion, in the results, of a certain beneficial effect of five or six years attendance at an American public school.

There is a very considerable difference between the central tendencies of the North Europeans and the South and East Europeans. Since the latter group is largely made up of Italians, the results merely show that the adding of other cases from Southern and Eastern Europe, still leaves the level of achievement much below that of the children of North European ancestry. It is to be noted that the standard deviations and probable errors of the means and medians are rather small for all of the groups, and that no significant increase in the reliability of the measures of central tendency would have been obtained by increasing the number of cases.

The differences in central tendency of the various groups is shown more clearly and in greater detail in table 22, which is derived from table 21. Each difference represents a subtraction of the central tendency of a group from that of the group to the left, indicated by a dash under the appropriate heading. In the case of the Illinois scores, the mean for the Finns subtracted from that for the Americans leaves 8.75, which is about three times, 2.73, its standard deviation. On the lower level, the mean for Italians lies about 26 points below the mean for the Americans, and the mean for French Canadians about 24 points below. That the gap between the two levels is not a matter of chance is shown by the fact that these differences are many times their standard deviation (146, 346). The differences in the case of Beta scores are much less marked, but the Americans and Finns exceed the Italians and the French Canadians taken as a group by amounts that are large compared with their standard deviations.

THE RESULTS COMPARED WITH NORMS

The question arises as to the standing of the groups studied, as compared with the children of the same age in the country at large. Reference to the table of mental ages and corresponding I.Q.'s in the handbook for the Illinois test reveals the equivalents of the mean point scores as given in table 23. It is apparent that the Americans stand somewhat higher than eleven-year-old children of the middle west, on whose scores the norms were based. On the other hand, the Finns have a mental age corresponding

TABLE 22

Differences between group central tendencies, and standard deviations of the differences of the means

Illinois scores

	AMERICANS			FINNS			ITALIANS			ALL FRENCH CANADIANS			A, FRENCH CANADIANS			B, FRENCH CANADIANS		
	Dif. Med.	Dif. M.	S.D. Dif. M.	Dif. Med.	Dif. M.	S.D. Dif. M.	Dif. Med.	Dif. M.	S.D. Dif. M.	Dif. Med.	Dif. M.	S.D. Dif. M.	Dif. Med.	Dif. M.	S.D. Dif. M.	Dif. Med.	Dif. M.	S.D. Dif. M.
	—	—	—	9.67	8.75	2.73	28.2	25.9	2.93	26.0	23.9	2.69	10.0	8.93	3.22	38.9	35.4	2.92
					—		18.5	17.2	2.58	16.4	15.11	2.31	0.33	0.18	2.9	29.3	26.7	2.6
								—		-2.2	-2.1	2.54	-18.2	-17.0	3.09	10.7	9.45	2.69
											—		-16.0	-14.9	2.87	12.9	11.5	2.44
														—		28.96	26.5	3.00

Beta scores

	AMERICANS			FINNS			ITALIANS			ALL FRENCH CANADIANS			A, FRENCH CANADIANS			B, FRENCH CANADIANS		
	Dif. Med.	Dif. M.	S.D. Dif. M.	Dif. Med.	Dif. M.	S.D. Dif. M.	Dif. Med.	Dif. M.	S.D. Dif. M.	Dif. Med.	Dif. M.	S.D. Dif. M.	Dif. Med.	Dif. M.	S.D. Dif. M.	Dif. Med.	Dif. M.	S.D. Dif. M.
	—	—	—	0.06	1.64	1.57	13.75	12.42	1.98	13.09	14.40	1.69	6.61	5.40	2.01	21.48	20.04	2.00
					—		13.69	10.78	1.85	13.03	12.76	1.55	6.55	3.76	1.88	21.42	18.40	1.88
								—		-0.66	1.98	1.96	-7.14	-7.02	2.23	7.73	7.62	2.22
											—		-6.48	-9.00	1.99	8.39	5.64	1.98
														—		14.87	14.64	2.25

almost exactly to their average chronological age of eleven and
a half years.   This corresponds to an I.Q. of 100, which of course is
not quite the same as their average I.Q., each I.Q. being figured
separately, but the difference is not great.   The French Canadians
taken as a group and the Italians have a standing only equal to
that of children a year or two younger.

There are no norms worked out for Beta as applied to school
children,[5] but it is interesting to compare the results for eleven-
year-olds with the results obtained by Young for twelve year
olds (145, 31).   The tests were administered in the same way and
the results are quite comparable.   As would be expected the mean
for the Massachusetts eleven-year-old Americans is lower than
the mean for California twelve-year-olds, being 65.83, as compared
with 68.30.   The Massachusetts Italians have a mean of 53.41,

TABLE 23

GROUP	MEAN SCORE	MENTAL AGE	I.Q.
American.....................................	67.17	12	104
Finns..	58.42	11–6	100
B. French Canadians.......................	31.76	8–6	74
A. French Canadians.......................	58.24	11–6	100
All French Canadians......................	43.31	10	87
Italians.....................................	41.21	9–6	83

as compared with 54.0, for the western Italians, so there is but a
slight difference in spite of the difference of a year in age.   The
Finns stand above all of the Latin groups studied by Young.
In general, the difference in age between the eastern and western
groups does not produce quite the difference in score that might
have been expected, yet the racial levels still stand out clearly
in both studes.

VARIABILITY

The differences in variability, as measured by the standard
deviation and semi-interquartile range of the distributions, are

[5] The Beta point scores would give rather low mental ages if converted
according to the Army Stanford-Binet equivalents, for according to these,
a Beta score of 74 only corresponds to a mental age of 11.5 (149, 133).

not as marked as the differences in central tendency. On the Illinois tests, as is apparent from table 21, only the two parochial schools A and B had standard deviations differing markedly from those of the other groups, in both cases, being somewhat lower. The Q of the B school is very low, but the Q of the A group is as high or higher than the others. The low standard deviation of the B group is due to the absence of high scores, in short, a concentration at the lower end of the scale. In the case of the A group, while there are few notably high scores, yet there is an absence of very low scores. In general, the conclusion would seem to be that, while the Americans are slightly superior, and the Italians and the two groups of French Canadians are slightly inferior in variability, no very significant differences exist in this respect.

On the Beta test differences in variability are somewhat greater, and tend to reverse the situation as shown by the Illinois test. The Finns and the Americans have approximately the same variability, as shown by both the standard deviation and the Q. The variability of the A French Canadians is still lower than that of the Americans and Finns, but that of the B French Canadians is considerably larger than that of the Americans and Finns, and is only exceeded by that of the French Canadians taken as a whole and by that of the Italians. It is significant that there is an increase in relative variability as well as in central tendency in the case of the B French Canadians and the Italians. It suggests that a non-language test shows better discrimination than a verbal test in groups which from other considerations would be expected to have the least perfect command of English.

The question arises, however, as to whether the American children were given full opportunity to manifest their capacities on Beta. Young in his study explains, in part, the slighter differences between Americans and Latins on Beta as compared with Alpha, by the assertion that the Beta tests did not discriminate at the higher level of intelligence of the American children (145, 59). The eleven-year-old children studied in this research, in contrast to the twelve-year-old children studied by Young, do not seem to be so handicapped. The distribution of the Beta scores is very normal and shows no piling up at the upper end of the scale. While it may be that Beta does not test the power of symbolic and conceptual thinking to the extent that the Illinois or other verbal tests do, yet there seems no evidence that the test scale failed to extend sufficiently far to allow variability full play. The increase in variability of the foreign-speaking groups can be as well or better explained by the hypothesis that the removal of a certain amount of linguistic handicap by the use of a non-verbal test allowed at least one aspect of intelligence full expression.

TABLE 24

Overlapping with respect to American quartiles

GROUP	Q. I.		MEDIAN		Q. III	
	Per cent above	Per cent below	Per cent above	Per cent below	Per cent above	Per cent below
Illinois						
Finns..........................	57.5	42.5	32.0	68.0	15.2	84.8
Italians........................	25.0	75.0	11.0	89.0	0	100.0
All French Canadians...........	28.5	71.5	15.0	85.0	0	100.0
A, French Canadians...........	55.0	45.0	35.2	64.8	7.0	93.0
B, French Canadians...........	10.5	89.5	0	100.0	0	100.0
Beta						
Finns..........................	71.2	28.8	50.0	50.0	23.0	77.0
Italians........................	35.0	65.0	19.0	81.0	12.0	88.0
All French Canadians...........	34.0	66.0	17.2	82.8	6.5	93.5
A, French Canadians...........	54.8	45.2	31.5	68.5	13.0	87.0
B, French Canadians...........	23.0	77.0	7.0	93.0	0	100.0

OVERLAPPING

A comparison of central tendencies, in many ways, does not give as adequate a picture of results as do facts as to overlapping. Overlapping of the Illinois scores is clearly brought out by figure 1 drawn from the percentiles of table 21. Likewise, table 24 gives the percentage of the various groups that exceed the first, second and third quartiles of the American distribution.[6] The ordinate

[6] In view of uncertain normality of distribution, the application of the Kelly (75) method of measurement of overlapping by the use of reliability coefficients seemed scarcely justified.

of the curves indicates the percentage of the total cases receiving a lower score than the corresponding abscissa.   The results of the study of central tendencies are confirmed by the curves of over-lapping, for it is apparent that there are two general levels of intelligence, that of the Americans, Finns and A French Cana-dians, and that of the other French Canadians and Italians. The Finnish distribution runs fairly parallel to that of the Ameri-

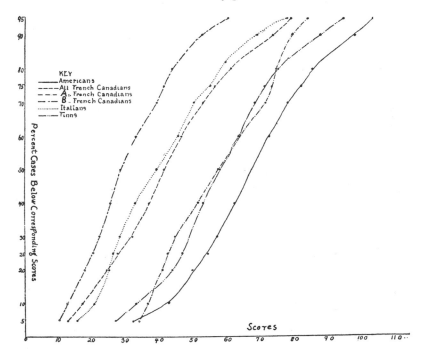

FIG. 1. CURVE OF OVERLAPPING ILLINOIS SCORES

cans, beginning and ending at a lower score.   At the American 25 percentile, there are 42.5 per cent of the Finns below, and 57.5 per cent above; 32 per cent exceed the American median, and but 15.2 per cent exceed the American third quartile.

About the same relation holds for the A French Canadians, save that the lower scores fail a trifle higher, and the overlapping is less at the higher quartiles, there being but 7 per cent that exceed the American third quartile. At an entirely different level, we find the French Canadians, taken as a group, although the form of distribution is much the same. There are a considerable number of low scores, in fact, 71.5 per cent of the cases lie below the first quartile of the Americans, but 15 per cent exceed the American median, and none lie above the American upper quartile. The Italians show even less overlapping in general, for 75 per cent are below the American first quartile, but 11 per cent exceed the American median, and none lie above the American upper quartile. The B French Canadians show by far the least overlapping. The concentration at low scores is very great, for 89.5 per cent lie below the American lower quartile and all are below the American median.

OVERLAPPING ON BETA

With respect to Beta scores, the overlapping is much greater but differences in achievement are still obvious and two general levels are maintained. On the upper level the Finns now overlap the Americans almost completely. We find that 71.2 per cent of the cases lie above the American lower quartile, 50 per cent lie above the median, and 23 per cent exceed the American upper quartile. Save for a few Americans that exceeded the highest scores of the Finnish children, the distributions are practically the same for both groups. The A group of French Canadians do not seem to profit by the change to a performance test to the same extent as do the Finns, for 45.2 per cent lie below the American lower quartile, but 31.5 per cent exceed the American median and only 13 per cent exceed the American third quartile. It would seem that they were less handicapped by the use of a verbal test than any other of the foreign-language groups. This is in accordance with the fact, to be brought out later, that a larger percentage used English in the home. Dragged down by the B group, and to some extent by the C group, the French Canadians taken as a whole maintain their position on the lower of the two levels of intelligence. There are 66 per cent of the cases below the American lower quartile, 17.2 per cent above the American median, and but 6.5 per cent above the American upper quartile. The status of the Italians, relative to the Americans, has improved very considerably by the use of a performance test. The improvement is not so much in lessening the number of lower scores, as in increasing the number of higher scores. Only 35 per cent exceed the American lower quartile and but 19 per cent exceed the median, yet there are 12 per cent above the upper quartile, almost as many as above the median. It is obvious

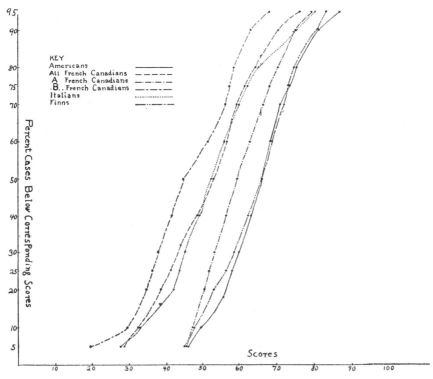

FIG. 2. CURVE OF OVERLAPPING BETA SCORES

that the performance test sets free the potential variability of the Italians and gives expression to capacities inhibited by the verbal test. In spite of the improvement shown, it is still clear that a wide gap exists between the achievement of the Italians and that of the Americans and the Finns. A similar improvement takes place in the standing of the B French Canadians on the performance test.   Only 23 per cent lie above the American lower quartile, yet 7 per cent exceed the American median, while none did this on the Illinois test.   The upper quartile of the Americans is still unattained.   The conclusion would seem to be that the Americans and Finns show a marked superiority to other groups even on the performance test.   The improved relative position of all foreign speaking groups indicates either, that the Americans were handicapped on Beta by its failure to measure the factor of mental power, previously mentioned, or that the foreign-speaking groups were handicapped on the Illinois test.   The latter hypothesis seems more valid, but the two propositions are not altogether mutually exclusive.

We have found very decided differences in the test achievement of the various national groups and some suggestion of a language handicap.   The next chapter will be devoted to the presentation of data that may aid in the interpretation of the findings.   In addition to the results of educational achievement tests, data bearing on the general environmental background of the different groups will be presented, and an analysis made of the evidence for a linguistic handicap.   This will lead to general conclusions as to the significance of the differences in test achievement as an indication of real differences in native intelligence.

CHAPTER IV

Interpretative Data, the Linguistic Handicap, Conclusions

RESULTS OF EDUCATIONAL ACHIEVEMENT TESTS

The educational achievement tests administered throw light on quantitative differences in native capacity, and also on the effect of environmental influences. Both achievement in arithmetic and in reading depend on intelligence, but it would be expected that reading achievement would be the more affected by facility in use of English, due to environmental conditions. The results are given in tables 25 and 26 in terms of achievement ages, that is to say, referred to the central tendency of corresponding age groups. An achievement age of twelve means that the number of points scored corresponds to the average score made by twelve year olds. The reading achievement age is derived from the average of achievement age, as determined by rate, and achievement age as determined by degree of comprehension, with the latter given double weight. The reliability of the means of the achievement ages is indicated by the P.E.'s of the means, which are invariably small.

The comparative achievement is about the same as in the case of the intelligence tests and it is probable that very much the same faculties are being tested. As Chapman (20), Toops (129), and others have shown, it is a question whether an educational test may be interpreted as measuring education, in contrast to measurement of native intelligence by an intelligence test. It is interesting that, while the Americans are over a year in advance of the other groups on reading achievement, they are exceeded in arithmetic by both the Finns and the A French Canadians, although the differences in the latter case are insignificant. As on the intelligence tests, the Finns compare rather favorably with the Americans, and show about an equal grade of achievement on both of the educational tests. The Italians show a slightly higher standing on the arithmetic tests than on the reading, but the improvement when tested with such non-verbal material is

77

not great, in fact, of little significance considering the size of the P.E.'s. This is in contrast to the marked improvement noted by Colvin (24). While the achievement of all of the French Canadians corresponded to the results of the mental tests, they did better on the arithmetic than on the reading test. In the case of the B French Canadians there is an improvement of almost a mental year on the arithmetic test over the reading test. This is significant, in view of the fact that this group suffered the most severe language handicap of any of the groups dealt with in this

TABLE 25
Reading ability of various groups

GROUP	NUMBER OF CASES	S.D. DIST.	MEAN A.A.	P.E. MEAN A.A.
Americans....................	93	2.81	13.48	0.196
Finns.........................	141	2.84	12.20	0.161
Italians......................	90	2.25	10.01	0.160
All French Canadians...........	151	2.54	10.05	0.139
A, French Canadians...........	52	2.57	11.71	0.241
B, French Canadians...........	71	2.06	8.99	0.165

TABLE 26
Ability of various groups in arithmetic

GROUP	NUMBER OF CASES	S.D. DIST.	MEAN A.A.	P.E. MEAN A.A.
American......................	91	1.52	12.0	0.107
Finns.........................	145	2.07	12.22	0.116
Italians......................	88	2.11	10.28	0.151
All French Canadians...........	156	2.08	10.90	0.112
A, French Canadians...........	53	3.49	12.31	0.324
B, French Canadians...........	75	2.99	9.90	0.234

study. The deficiencies of the group in command of English were clearly apparent from observation during the administration of the tests.

The evidence from the achievement tests is perhaps more clearly brought out by a consideration of achievement quotients as presented in table 27. The achievement quotient is the quotient derived by dividing the achievement age by the mental age. It is supposed to measure the school achievement, in relation to the endowment of intelligence, which makes achievement possible.

The reading achievement quotient is the average of the quotient for rate and for comprehension. The means and medians are presented for both arithmetic and reading A.Q.'s but since the distributions are frequently much skewed, the two measures of central tendency differ by considerable amounts. The differences in central tendency for the two types of performance are also presented in table 27. These differences are obtained by subtracting the average arithmetic A.Q. from the average reading A.Q., and hence a minus sign indicates that the reading A.Q. is less than the arithmetic A.Q. For the French Canadian groups the differences tend to be minus, and likewise in the case of the Italians, the arithmetic A.Q. is slightly greater than the

TABLE 27

Central tendencies of A.Q.'s and differences in C. T. between reading A.Q. and arithmetic A.Q.

GROUP	C.T. READING A.Q.		C.T. ARITHMETIC A.Q.		DIFFERENCES IN C.T.	
	Median	Mean	Median	Mean	Median	Mean
Americans	112.94	111.05	95.93	107.0	17.01	4.05
Finns	104.16	106.76	103.64	105.15	0.52	1.61
Italians	102.84	106.20	104.46	104.75	−1.62	1.45
All French Canadians	95.55	102.6	108.33	107.9	12.78	−5.30
A, French Canadians	103.20	108.60	105.25	108.40	−2.05	0.20
B, French Canadians	99.23	102.05	108.33	109.40	−9.10	−7.35

reading A.Q. The Finnish group shows little difference in the A.Q.'s. The Americans, however, do far better in reading in relation to their intelligence, as measured by the Illinois test, than they do in arithmetic.

The facts suggest that some of the foreign groups are handicapped in about the same proportion on both the reading and the verbal intelligence tests, while their capacities are given freer play on the arithmetic tests. On the other hand, the Americans, who enjoy perfect facility in use of English, have a very high standing in both reading and intelligence test achievement, while relative to the latter, the performance in arithmetic is not so creditable. This view is opposed by the facts as to the Finns, whose environment would seem to make for as great a handicap as in the case of the other immigrant groups. There is doubtless truth in the contention that native intelligence lies back of facility in the manipulation of verbal material and it seems that the high intelligence of the Finns, which has made possible effective performance in both reading and arithmetic, has wiped out differences that might have been apparent had nature controlled nurture less effectively.

SOCIAL AND ECONOMIC STATUS

In view of the necessity for careful control of environmental factors before differences or resemblances can be explained entirely in terms of innate characteristics, it seemed advisable to collect as much data as possible concerning the social and economic status of the families from which the children came.

A questionnaire was given to the children with questions as to the work of the father, the number of rooms in the home, and the number of persons living in them. The method is open to objections of various kinds but the faults tend to be of omission rather than of commission. It was impossible to obtain satisfactory data in all of the cases, but that which was obtained may be considered as quite free from misrepresentation. The errors would lie in possible selective influences determining which children gave data complete enough to use. The more intelligent in all groups would tend to give more complete data, but since this selective influence would work in the same direction for all groups, the differences between the portions of the groups that gave satisfactory data must be considered as fairly representative of differences between the groups as a whole. The facts as to occupation of the father may be put in terms of the Taussig classification (123, 134–8). Class I of the five-fold scale includes the unskilled day laborer, Class II the semi-skilled, Class III the skilled workman. Class IV represents the lower middle class, consisting of clerks, foremen, proprietors of small businesses, and the like. Class V consists of the higher-middle class such as professional or business men, officials, etc. Since the fathers of many of the children were employed in textile mills, expert advice was obtained as to the degree of skill required in the various tasks. The classification is not intended to take into account the intelligence required for a given occupation, but it would show a rough correspondence to the occupational levels worked out by Fryer (43).

The percentages of the total number of children who gave complete data whose fathers are in each class, are listed in table 28 with the standard deviation of the distribution among the classes, the mean of the distribution, and the probable error of the mean. In general the results confirm the findings of Pressey (99), Bridges (14) and Arlitt (3) and indicate that a relation exists between the intelligence of a group and its social status. The relationship is by no means perfect for the Finns are lower in

TABLE 28

Social status as indicated by the occupation of father rated by the Taussig scale

GROUP	NUMBER OF CASES	PER CENT IN CLASS I	PER CENT IN CLASS II	PER CENT IN CLASS III	PER CENT IN CLASS IV	PER CENT IN CLASS V	STANDARD DEVIATION	MEAN	P.E. MEAN
Americans	82	2.44	18.3	33.0	24.4	22.0	1.09	3.45	0.081
Finns	109	5.5	56.1	29.4	8.3	0.9	0.76	2.43	0.049
Italians	60	20.0	48.3	20.7	11.7	0	0.91	2.25	0.079
All French Canadians	97	6.17	43.3	36.0	13.4	1.0	0.83	2.60	0.057
A, French Canadians	32	0	50.0	34.4	12.5	3.1	0.81	2.69	0.095
B, French Canadians	41	12.2	29.2	46.3	12.2	0	0.70	2 59	0.074

social status and the B French Canadians higher than might have been expected from the test results.

While this relation must be taken into account before assuming that the differences in achievement on intelligence tests are entirely due to native intelligence, yet it by no means follows that, for a fair comparison of groups, only those of the same social status should be considered. All that can be asked is that a representative sample of the occupational distribution for the various nationalities be obtained. To select Americans of the same social status for comparison with immigrant groups would in all probability mean a selection from the lower end of the scale of distribution of native abilities among the Americans. Whether reflecting superior intelligence of the parent, or favorable strategic position born of long residence in this country, the occupations of the fathers of the American children certainly rank much higher on the scale than do those of any of the other groups. Over a fifth are in Class V and there are almost none in Class I. The French Canadians rank somewhat higher than do the Finns, which suggests the influence of longer residence in this country The A group rank slightly above the B group, but not by an amount that can be considered as significant. As might be expected from recency of arrival and intellectual status, the Italians rank lowest of all, having a fifth of the total in Class I and none in Class V.

The use of housing conditions as an index of economic status does not depend on an arbitrary classification, as does occupational

TABLE 29

Social status as indicated by number of rooms per person

GROUP	NUMBER OF CASES	MEAN	P.E. MEAN	STANDARD DEVIATION
Americans....................	86	1.32	0.065	0.603
Finns........................	136	1.02	0.026	0.452
Italians......................	71	0.82	0.036	0.382
All French Canadians..........	105	0.85	0.026	0.398
A, French Canadians..........	27	0.97	0.063	0.490
B, French Canadians..........	51	0.75	0.030	0.317

data, although there are other objections. The number of rooms per person for the different nationalities is given in table 29. While this reflects economic status, it is affected by the prevailing size of family. The table shows that the group differences are more marked, but the same order exists save that the Finns now rank next to the Americans. The differences between the A and the B French Canadians are rather striking, and in view of the small size of the probable errors, must be considered as having some significance. The mean number of rooms per person is of course affected by the size of family, as is shown by a correlation with the number of living children to be found on the average in the homes of the different nationalities studied.

Further study of environment would probably tend to confirm that which is suggested by the data given; namely that the Americans rank first as to favorable social environment, followed by the Finns and French Canadians, and finally by the Italians who take lowest place. While these differences must be kept in mind in interpreting the test results, it should be remembered that the intelligence of the stock may affect both social status and test performance.

THE CORRELATIONS

The correlations worked out by the Pearson method between the results of the various tests and other variables are given in table 30. The correlation between the scores on the Illinois tests and on the Beta test is fairly high for all groups. In the case of Americans, French Canadians and Finns the coefficients are of very nearly the same size, while for the Italians it is a trifle higher. These correlations are about as high as those obtained by Young (145, 49) between Alpha and Beta scores, and they compare favorably with the correlations between most group tests, especially when one is of the verbal and the other of the performance type (50). As Gates (47) points out, correlations are affected by the amount of non-verbal material which two tests have in common. Stated more broadly, correlations depend on the degree to which equal weight is given, in the two tests, to each of the factors of intelligence. It is significant that these two tests of decidedly different type measure that which we know as general intelligence, in a sufficiently accurate fashion to give a fair degree of correspondence. In all cases the coefficients are many times the probable error, and must be regarded as being reliable to a high degree.

Perhaps the best outside criterion, by which the validity of tests as measuring learning capacity may be checked up, is grade location. It is of course true that personality and other non-intellectual traits may affect grade location, but in general retardation or advancement is a fairly good indication of the amount of native intelligence. The correlations of Illinois with grade location are about as great as the correlations of Illinois with Beta, and may be taken to show that the standing as to test score really indicates in a significant way the capacity of a child for education. For all of the groups the correlations of Illinois with grade loca-

TABLE 30

Correlations Pearson method with achievement age

GROUP	r WITH BETA SCORES	r WITH ACHIEVE-MENT AGE IN READING	r WITH GRADE LOCATION	r WITH OCCUPATION OF FATHER	r WITH NUMBER OF ROOMS PER PERSON	r WITH ACHIEVE-MENT AGE IN ARITHMETIC
Americans:						
Illinois scores.........	0.65 ± 0.04	0.56 ± 0.05	0.61 ± 0.04	0.23 ± 0.06	0.25 ± 0.07	0.57 ± 0.04
Beta scores...........		0.38 ± 0.06	0.57 ± 0.05	0.17 ± 0.07		0.46 ± 0.06
Finns:						
Illinois scores.........	0.65 ± 0.04	0.72 ± 0.03	0.67 ± 0.03	0.30 ± 0.06	0.03 ± 0.06	0.75 ± 0.02
Beta scores...........		0.39 ± 0.05	0.54 ± 0.04	0.13 ± 0.06		0.62 ± 0.03
All of French Canadians:						
Illinois scores.........	0.64 ± 0.03	0.62 ± 0.03	0.65 ± 0.03	0.16 ± 0.07	0.12 ± 0.06	0.68 ± 0.03
Beta scores...........		0.35 ± 0.05	0.62 ± 0.03	0.29 ± 0.06		0.69 ± 0.03
Italians:						
Illinois scores.........	0.73 ± 0.03	0.71 ± 0.04	0.85 ± 0.02	0.32 ± 0.08	0.00	0.76 ± 0.03
Beta scores...........		0.55 ± 0.05	0.65 ± 0.04	0.22 ± 0.08		0.65 ± 0.04

tion were 0.60 or more, which is as large or larger than is usually obtained (72). The correlations of Beta against grade location were smaller in every case, but still indicate that a fair degree of predictability is possible by use of a performance test. It might be argued that, since Illinois correlates higher with grade location than does Beta, the difficulties due to its verbal character are insignificant, and that it really measures innate learning capacity, and especially the faculties of symbolic thinking that are indispensable to continued school progress. This is true in part, but it should be remembered that the common factor of language handicap might affect both the score on the verbal test and the grade location.

There is a slight correlation between the intelligence of the children and the occupation of the parent but much less than that obtained by Dexter (35). The correlation might have been considerably raised had the occupational classification been more elaborate. In the case of intelligence and the housing index, the correlation was still lower, but special studies of this relation show that it is ordinarily only about 0.25 (22). The important thing is the fact, that the relation between social status of groups and their average intelligence which we have found to exist, also holds to a certain extent for individuals within the groups. The question of which variable is cause and which effect must be left undecided, although it is probable that the relation is reciprocal.

In every group the correlation of Illinois scores with reading achievement is higher than in the case of Beta, perhaps due to the common factor of language involved.[1] The Illinois test also correlated higher with arithmetic than did Beta, although the differences are not so great. Probably therefore, the Illinois examination tests verbal facility, but also tests the power factor in intelligence involving conceptual thinking, to a greater extent than is done by Beta. Since in the case of the American children, the correlation of intelligence with educational achievement tests is lower than that for other groups, this may indicate that the school work assigned is less adapted to their intelligence.

[1] Gates found that, in general, the more verbal the test, the higher the correlation with school achievement (48).

THE POSSIBLE LANGUAGE HANDICAP

In the previous discussion there has been some suggestion of the existence of a language handicap arising out of: 1, improved relative standing of certain of the immigrant groups with the use of a performance test, 2, a tendency to increased variability under these conditions, 3, differential performance on reading and arithmetic tests. It is now necessary to deal directly with this problem and in so doing two points brought out in the first chapter will be found useful.

First, differences between individuals or groups may only be considered hereditary when the significant aspects of environment are constant. In general, the environmental factors are much more constant in this research than in the case of the army testing. Almost all of the children are born in this country and have had several years of instruction in the schools, carried on in English. For the children of immigrant groups, other conditions tend to be much the same, especially the general use of the foreign language in the home. Therefore when we have great differences in the performance of Italians and Finns it is very difficult to explain such differences on environmental or linguistic grounds. Such differences are weighty evidence that test achievement really corresponds to intelligence. All of the foreign groups however, differ from the American children in the use of a language other than English in the home and it is necessary to consider whether children may not suffer a relative handicap even after several years of instruction carried on in English. The work of Saer (112) (113) and Smith (116) suggests that bilingualism is a handicap even when there is no distinct lack of familiarity with the language used in the test.

In the second place it was pointed out that any classification by intelligence tests involves a certain arbitrary weighting or evaluation of the factors that enter into intelligence such as versatility, speed, intellectual power. For this reason it is hard to say whether poor performance in connection with verbal material indicates a deficiency in one aspect of intelligence, such as intellectual power, or whether that power is potential but baulked by linguistic difficulties. Likewise an equality of performance on a non-verbal test may not eliminate the possibility of differences in aspects of intelligence that are not brought into play. It is unlikely that in the case of Beta or other performance tests the factors of power and versatility are tested to the same extent as by verbal tests.

With these points in mind, we may first, investigate the relationship of the language used in the home to test performance, and second, make a detailed analysis of the sub-tests that make up the Illinois and Beta tests as a whole, comparing achievement on verbal and non-verbal material. Finally we may look for evidence that linguistic factors are involved, in the difference in test performance of the A and B groups of French Canadians.

RELATION BETWEEN TEST ACHIEVEMENT AND LANGUAGE USED IN THE HOME

The evidence pointing to an accentuation of differences in intelligence by a language handicap is derived by the aid of the coefficient of mean-square-contingency. This is a statistical device differing from a coefficient of correlation, in that it measures the degree of association between attributes, rather than between continuous variables. The formula given by Rugg (111, 304–305) was used. In essence the formula determines the degree to which the association of attributes deviates from a purely chance association. A coefficient approaching the value 1.00 would indicate an almost perfect association over and above that which would be expected by pure chance. The range of test scores on both Illinois and Beta were divided into five classes, and a calculation made to determine the association of these ratings with three attributes; namely, 1, sole use of English in the home in speaking with both parents, 2, use of both English and the foreign tongue in the home, and 3, the use of only the foreign language in the home. The question is, whether there is an association between the use of English in the home and the level of achievement on the tests. The results are given in table 31 and show that a rather decided relationship exists. It is to be noted that in every case, save that of the Finns, the coefficient for Illinois scores and use of English is higher than that for Beta scores. That it is not true also for the Finns, is probably to be explained by the fact that, although they were a group of considerable size, a very small proportion of them spoke other than the parental language in the home, thus making the coefficient of mean-square-contingency very uncertain as to validity. But 3 out of the 130 that gave satisfactory data spoke only English in the home, although about 30 spoke both English and Finnish.

In the case of the A French Canadians, out of the 46 that gave data, 7 spoke both French and English and 9 spoke only English. In the case of the B French Canadians who took the Illinois test, and who gave satisfactory data, only 4 out of 50 spoke both languages, and 8, English alone. If the same percentage of the B group had given data as it gave in the A group there is no doubt

TABLE 31

Coefficients of mean-square-contingency showing relation of, use of foreign language, use of foreign language and English, and use of English alone, to test score

GROUP	ILLINOIS		BETA	
	Number of cases	Coef.	Number of cases	Coef.
Finns............................	130	0.260	130	0.395
Italians.........................	76	0.516	82	0.252
All French Canadians.............	118	0.490	125	0.269
A, French Canadians.............	46	0.650	46	0.291
B, French Canadians.............	50	0.427	58	0.381

that the proportion speaking other than French would have been much less, for a selective influence operated whereby those with a good knowledge of English were more likely to answer the question in a satisfactory manner. There is little doubt that taking the B group as a whole, the use of English was much less frequent than in the case of the A French Canadians. In the case of the Italians, 20 out of 76 spoke partly English, and 8, English alone, which is roughly about the same proportion as in the case of A French Canadians.

It might be expected that the coefficient for the B group, with the apparent language difficulty, would be higher than that for the A French Canadians. It is not certain, however, that an extreme depressing effect of one variable upon another would tend

TABLE 32
Mean scores on sub-tests and per cent receiving low scores

GROUP	TEST I Mean	Per cent 0-2	TEST II Mean	Per cent 0-2	TEST III Mean	Per cent 0-2	TEST IV Mean	Per cent 0-3	TEST V Mean	Per cent 0-2	TEST VI Mean	Per cent 0-2	TEST VII Mean	Per cent 0-2
Illinois test														
Americans..............	8.68	11.7	7.88	0	11.9	1.1	14.4	2.2	10.5	1.1	9.44	0	7.7	18.7
Finns..................	7.04	22.2	7.71	2.0	9.69	4.7	13.6	4.1	9.9	0.66	8.78	3.9	5.72	19.7
Italians...............	3.02	41.7	5.56	7.3	5.88	20.9	10.9	19.0	7.7	1.03	7.62	3.1	3.03	56.2
All French Canadians...	4.52	34.2	6.26	9.5	6.02	19.5	10.98	14.2	8.05	5.15	7.54	5.15	4.73	37.2
A, French Canadians....	6.04	13.4	8.38	1.9	8.40	1.9	13.04	15.4	9.88	2.0	8.40	2.0	7.40	18.0
B, French Canadians....	3.15	50.0	5.05	14.9	4.22	37.8	9.31	17.8	7.16	6.9	6.86	8.2	3.14	52.0
Beta test														
Americans..............	3.17	6.5	7.74	3.26	10.1	0	14.7	0	15.6	0	12.0	0	5.18	7.46
Finns..................	3.29	5.8	7.14	3.6	9.85	0.72	14.8	0	15.4	0	11.7	0.70	5.51	2.12
Italians...............	2.57	23.4	6.28	8.5	8.64	0	12.2	5.26	14.0	3.16	9.15	0	3.57	14.8
All French Canadians...	2.66	22.0	5.93	13.4	8.11	3.66	11.4	3.6	13.3	4.9	10.4	3.7	3.21	18.5
A, French Canadians....	2.84	24.0	5.33	16.3	9.78	2.04	14.9	0	15.5	0	11.3	0	4.15	10.9
B, French Canadians....	2.51	21.3	6.35	12.5	6.85	6.2	9.0	6.1	12.2	7.4	9.63	0	3.06	21.2

to cause a more intimate relationship between the two.   Further-more, the fact that a smaller percentage of the B group gave the data requested may have had some influence.

Finally the question arises as to why, if the Beta be a non-language test, a relation appeared between Beta scores and the language used in the home.   For one thing, the correlation of Beta with Illinois would cause it also to be associated with the use of English.   Also it is conceivable that the parents using English acquired it because of superior intelligence which they passed on to their children to be manifested on Beta scores.   In general the evidence seems to be to the effect that Illinois scores are affected by the linguistic situation in the home.

ANALYSIS OF THE ILLINOIS SUB-TESTS

The mean scores made by the different groups on the various sub-tests of the Illinois examination are presented in table 32, together with the percentage of each group making low scores on each sub-test.   The significance of the data is more readily ap-parent when presented in graphic form as in figure 3.   The or-dinate represents the mean scores of the various sub-tests indicated by number at the bottom.   Instead of being arranged in numerical series the tests are grouped so that the first four tests are those more dependent on language, while the last three are those which are less verbal in type.

While the profile graphs run parallel in a general way, reflecting the weight attached to the various sub-tests and their comparative difficulty for all groups, still the difference in achievement of the various groups is much greater on some of the tests than on others. There is no denying the fact that the superiority of the Americans is chiefly on the verbal tests.   Test I is an analogies test made up of propositions, as for example, "sailor is to navy as soldier is to ——," and here the word army, rather than gun, private or fight, should be underlined.   Undoubtedly this depends on more than mere verbal fluency, and yet a quick perception of the mean-ing of words born of an English speaking environment and a home life in which books play a part, must be considered an asset, and the lack of such, a handicap.   On this test the Italians do

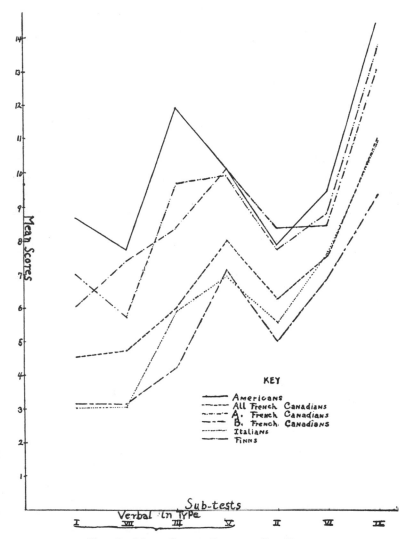

FIG. 3. MEAN SCORES ILLINOIS SUB-TESTS

only about a third as well as the Americans. The same is true of the B French Canadians. The Finns and the A French Canadians, while making fairly high absolute scores, stand considerably lower in relation to the Americans on this test than on those less verbal in character.

The next test, which is VII on the examination blank, is a synonym-antonym test depending even more on vocabulary. There is no doubt that ability to acquire a knowledge of the meanings of words, where the environment makes possible such an acquirement, is to be considered a part of general intelligence. However, when the environment is not the same, differences in command of word meanings cannot be considered a sure indication of lack of intelligence. It is likely that a child of ignorant Italian parents, hearing nothing but Italian in the home, and receiving scant encouragement in the use of library books, would have difficulty in determining whether "tease" and "plague" meant the same or the opposite. It is true that, if the Finns under similar conditions show little handicap, they must be considered superior in intelligence to the Italians. However, the educational tradition may have been more favorable, since the Finns are far more likely to be literate. It is also quite probable that with an American environment they might have done even better.

Test III still finds the B French Canadians and the Italians doing only about a half as well as the Americans, while the Finns and the A French Canadians stand lower relative to the Americans, than they do on other tests. It is a vocabulary and information test in which it is asked, whether a guitar is used to make toys, glass, music or furniture, and on the more difficult levels of this power test it is required to tell whether ambergris is used in candles, fishing, medicine or perfumery.

Test V of verbal ingenuity, while depending on reading ability, makes ingenuity far more important than language facility. Such words as "brown the horse come is," must be rearranged to form a sentence, in this case, "the horse is brown," by crossing out the extra word, "come." On this test the Finns and A French Canadians equalled the American performance and the other curves approach the American level as closely as in the case of the non-verbal tests.

Test II, an arithmetic test, is the first of the three grouped together as being more distinctly non-verbal in type. Comprehension of the problems depends on ability to read simple material but there is little reason to think that any, save perhaps the B French Canadians, could have found this much of an obstacle. Test VI is less dependent on language than any of the others, once the directions are grasped. A series of numbers is given, such as 2, 4, 6, 7, 8, one of which does not fit in the series and is to be crossed out, in this case 7. On this test the differences between the various groups are less than on any other of the subtests, although the rank order is about the same and real differences of ability undoubtedly exist. It should be noted that this test, while non-verbal, still places considerable demand on intellectual power in the sense of capacity for analysis and ability to perceive abstract relationships. The last of the three non-verbal tests, listed as IV on the examination blank, is a substitution test in which numbers are placed beside appropriate symbols. Once the idea is grasped it is merely a test of rapidity in forming simple associations. While the absolute mean scores are high, due to the system of weighting, the graphs show considerable differences in achievement. The Americans, Finns and the A French Canadians stand very close together. On a lower level we find the Italians and the French Canadians taken as a group, and still lower, the B French Canadians.

The data of table 32 showing the percentage in each group receiving zero or very low scores, have been converted and presented in figure 4. Instead of giving the percentage receiving the low scores, the percentage of cases above the stated low scores is used as the ordinate, thus making easier the comparison with the graph just discussed. As might be expected, the relative position of the lines corresponds to the curves showing mean scores. On the first three tests, chiefly verbal, the curves are separated as in figure 3, save that the upper group of lines lie rather close together. The curves all approach each other quite closely on the last four tests. It is of course obvious that a considerable percentage of extremely low scores, most of them zero, would lower the mean scores, and the common cause would seem to be a language handicap that practically inhibited achievement. This went hand in hand with, and was partly caused by inferior intelligence. It is not likely that there was any chance misunderstanding of the directions for the general shape of the curve is

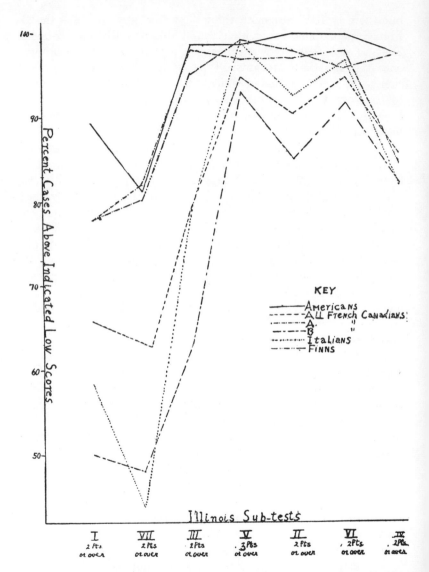

FIG. 4.   PER CENT CASES ABOVE THE INDICATED LOW SCORES ON ILLINOIS
SUB-TESTS

the same for all groups, even for the Americans. It is unlikely that all would misunderstand the directions for the same tests.

Therefore the general conclusion to be drawn from the results is that on a typically verbal test, the children of immigrant parents tend to be handicapped to a certain extent because of an inadequate linguistic background. The analysis of sub-tests shows just as clearly, however, that differences even on non-verbal material exist, that can best be explained by differences in intelligence as it has been defined, and not by environmental factors alone.

It would be expected from the preceding that the means of the sub-tests of the Beta examination would show a fairly close correspondence for the various groups, since they are all of the performance type. Figure 5 shows this to be the case. While the general levels are maintained, the curves tend to run more parallel than did those for the Illinois examination. The per cent of the means for the Americans, by which the means for the other groups differ, is fairly constant and is smaller than in the case of Illinois. The greatest differences in mean score are on tests IV and V, the former being a substitution test and the latter one requiring the recognition of difference or likeness between pairs of numbers of increasing size. Neither is based on language and the differences in achievement are probably due to differences in native ability. The conclusion then is that differences in native ability exist, which are merely accentuated on a verbal test by a language handicap.

The same points can be brought out in another way, and in perhaps a more concise fashion than by graphic presentation. If four Beta sub-tests be selected which seem least dependent on language, and if from the sum of the partial scores made on these tests by each child, there be subtracted the sum of the partial scores on the four most verbal tests of the Illinois examination, the difference gives a fair index of differential achievement on non-verbal and verbal material. The medians of the differences found for individual children in particular groups may be compared. For the Americans the median difference was 11.87, for

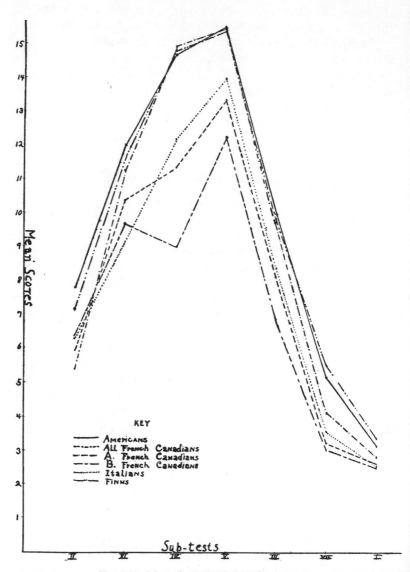

KEY
———— Americans
—·—·— All French Canadians
—··—··— A. French Canadians
—·—·— B. French Canadians
··········· Italians
——— Finns

FIG. 5.   MEN SCORES, BETA SUB-TESTS

the A French Canadians it was 14.77. For the Italians the median difference was 23.86 and in the case of the B French Canadians, who from observation and indirect evidence, had a most scanty command of English, the median difference was 24.17. The contrast between the medians is very striking, but it tends to be lessened by the fact that the differences between larger numbers, while perhaps not large relative to the size of the numbers involved, may seem large because of the magnitude of the minuend and subtrahend. To control this, the sums of the partial scores for the two tests were put in terms of the per cent of the total scores that these sums of the selected partial scores represented. The differences of the percentages were then found and the medians of the differences were determined for the various groups. In short the median is taken of the various values of the formula.

$$\frac{\text{sum, 2, 4, 5, 6, Beta. 100}}{\text{Total Beta score}} - \frac{\text{sum, 1, 3, 5, 7, Ill. 100}}{\text{Total Illinois score}}$$

rather than values of: sum, 2, 4, 5, 6, Beta—sum, 1, 3, 5, 7, Illinois, as previously. The median for the Americans is now 15.50; for the A French Canadians 26.39, for the Italians 33, 74, and for the B French Canadians 38.12. It is apparent that according to this method of calculation the results are equally striking. The most distinctly foreign-speaking groups do relatively much better on non-verbal than verbal material, and this suggests an influence of linguistic environment over and above any possible innate deficiency in the power aspect of intelligence. The language handicap adds differences due to nurture to any basic differences in average group intelligence.

THE DIFFERENCES BETWEEN FRENCH CANADIAN GROUPS

It is appropriate to consider at this point the problem offered by the striking difference in standing of the A and the B parochial schools. It is only in the case of French Canadians that there is an indication of lack of homogeneity and this anomalous situation is open to three explanations. On the one hand it is possible that the two schools have populations that actually differ widely in native intelligence and it is this difference in native intelligence that is reflected in the test results. If there were frequently such large differences in the apparent abilities of two groups, both sufficiently large to give small probable errors for the means, doubt is cast on the possibility of selecting representative sample of a class or nationality from an entire population. Fifty or a hundred beans picked at random from a bin containing thousands would only represent the total, when either the selection is made from many different levels in the bin, or when the beans have been so mixed that the entire mass is homogeneous as to the prevailing size of bean. If three samples are taken in which the beans show marked difference in average size, it is uncertain which gives a true picture of the entire mass. The sampling for intelligence among French Canadians may, by analogy, be such as to render reasoning from the particular to the universal an uncertain procedure. However, as we have seen, the other groups seem to be representative samples of homogeneous populations, at least in so far as one section of the country is concerned.

Another possibility is that the native ability of both of the sub-groups is roughly the same and that the differences in test performance are due to differences arising out of environmental conditions, especially differential facility in the use and comprehension of the English language. If this should be the correct explanation, the implications are hostile to the view that intelligence tests are valid instruments for the measurement of native intelligence regardless of environmental conditions. A third possibility is that both causes contribute to the result, which is to assume that the B children are less intelligent than the A children and have their dullness accentuated by a language handicap and inferior educational advantages. To accept this view is to sacrifice force and conclusiveness, but it probably means a closer approach to the truth of the matter. It is a main point of the entire discussion that no absolutely conclusive decision can be made concerning problems of nature and nurture until the variables have been completely controlled and this is very difficult in dealing with human material.

It is perhaps well in the first place to sum up the points suggesting that differences in intelligence as defined, exist between the two main French Canadian groups: 1, The differences in grade location are suggestive of true differences in ability when, as in this case, the mean grade location differs by four-fifths of a grade, even when there is reason to believe that the standards for grade assignment are lower rather than higher in the B school. 2, Again, the C results like those for the B school indicate an inferior intellectual status, and in this case the environment was that of a public school. Two of the three sub-samples then, give a low standing to the French Canadians, even when the two samples are from different types of school. 3, Furthermore in both C and B schools, children were pointed out by the teachers whom they pronounced to be distinctly feeble-minded. The diagnosis in these cases was borne out by personal observation when giving the tests and by the extremely low scores, even on Beta. 4, In the A school on the contrary, no such cases were noted and the distribution of scores owes its slight variability to the absence of distinctly low scores. There is some reason to think that in this school some selection has taken place and that inferior children are likely to be relegated to the public schools. 5, Data as to birth place of parents and children has some bearing on the possibility of selection as well as on cultural characteristics. About four-fifths of the A children gave data on these points as compared with two-thirds for the B group. Of those giving data a little more than a third had both parents born in Canada and a sixth had both parents born in the United States, with the rest of mixed parentage. Only two of the children were born in Canada. In the case of the B group, of those giving data, 39, or about two-thirds had both parents born in Canada, while but 6, or about one-tenth, had both parents born in the United States, the rest being of mixed birth. There were 8 of the children themselves who reported that they were born in Canada, in contrast to 2 for the A group. It is apparent that, although the movement of French Canadians to Fitchburg was a little earlier than that to Leominster, the B group of children is of a stock more recent in arrival. It is probable that if the returns from the B group had been more complete the proportion having parents born in Canada would have been increased. There is a possibility that a certain selection has taken place, of the kind that often occurs, and the best stock has been the first to migrate. 6, There is some evidence of a difference in the place of origin of the two groups, for the questionnaire data showed a greater proportion from New Brunswick rather than Quebec, in the B as compared with the A group. Priest and teachers both voluntarily, and on being questioned, confirmed the fact of a greater proportion of such emigrants among the stock making up the parents of the B group of children. 7, The most important evidence for real differences in intelligence between the two groups is to be found in the Beta scores. No matter how the comparison is made, the A group is far superior on every single sub-test. It is not at all likely that by interchanging the environments of the two groups the ranking on this test would be changed.

Turning to the environmental factor, however, there is considerable evidence to show that the differences, especially on the Illinois tests, are much greater than differences in native intelligence can account for. 1, The facts as to the language used in the home are significant, for 16 of the A group as compared with 12 for the B group used English partly or entirely in the home. Furthermore as has been pointed out, those of the B group that failed to give data are likely to have used only French, thus the proportion using English is doubtless really less than is indicated by the incomplete data. 2, All of the evidence cited to show that the B group on the average tended to be newer to the environment of the United States, points to a possible cultural handicap. In the case of the children themselves, at least 8 were born in Canada and there were 3 others who had just come to school, probably from Canada, and knew almost no English. 3, Observation of the children while they took the tests, and the difficulties they experienced in writing simple answers to the questionnaire, all pointed to a very limited knowledge of English. 4, The general lack of facility in English was both a cause and effect of the obviously inferior educational situation in the B school. Handicapped by the character of the school population, by overcrowding and an insufficient teaching staff, the school had succeeded only to a slight extent in giving the pupils an education corresponding to their age and grade. While the teachers and especially the Principal were themselves of English origin, intelligent and competent, yet it was apparent that the obstacles were too great to permit them to achieve the best results in education and assimilation. If Burt (18) be correct in stressing the degree to which mental tests reflect education, we have a partial explanation of the poor scores made by the B children on the Illinois test. 5, The sociological situation in the case of the B children is probably of some effect. There is great concentration in a single district, of the French Canadian population of the city, so that the French language is used constantly even by the children at play, the general effect being imperfect assimilation as compared with the A children who are less isolated. 6, As we have seen the educational tests give a rough index of language handicap, and by this index the B and the A groups differ markedly. The achievement age in arithmetic for the B children is about a year higher than the achievement age in reading, a greater difference than the A children show on these two tests. In arithmetic the B group approaches the standing of the A group more closely than it does in reading. The difference in A.Q. in favor of arithmetic is greater for the B than for the A group, all of which suggests that the B group experienced linguistic handicaps to a greater extent than the A children. 7, For the most direct and convincing evidence of environmental conditions as a partial cause of the difference in the standing of the two French Canadian groups, we must turn to the tests themselves. We find that when Beta results are considered, that the gap between the two groups which was so great in the case of the Illinois scores has closed up to a considerable extent. Furthermore a consideration of partial scores on the Illinois tests shows that on the verbal elements the B children stand much lower compared with the A group than on the non-verbal tests. We must conclude from the total evidence that both nature and nurture have collaborated to produce the differences in performance between the French Canadian groups.

SUMMARY AND GENERAL CONCLUSIONS

1. Following a discussion of methods and materials, estimates of intelligence for a limited number of children from the various groups were presented, which indicated that the Finns and Ameri-

cans were considered by the teachers to be about equally superior to the Italians.

2. The Finns in a large high school received academic honors out of proportion to their numbers, and grammar school marks indicated considerable superiority of the Finns and Americans over the Italians.

3. Americans, Finns and A French Canadians have about the same mean grade location, but that of the first two groups would have been higher if wider variation were allowed. The French Canadians, taken as a group, on the average stand slightly lower than the Americans and Finns. The Italians, who like the latter attend the public schools, have a mean grade location about a grade below the American or Finnish children.

4. An analysis of nationality achievement by schools showed similarity of average school scores thus indicating homogeneity of the samples, save in the case of the French Canadians. Since two schools differed widely in achievement, these main subgroups in the French Canadian sample were treated separately. The differences between the French Canadian schools were not merely due to the number of cases since considerable numbers of children discarded because of wrong age showed the same differences, the factor of age being taken into account. A miscellaneous group of North Europeans stood above a miscellaneous group of South and East Europeans. The latter group, however, approached the average score for their age according to test norms.

5. A comparison of the central tendencies of the distributions of the Illinois scores showed notable differences. The Americans with a mean score of 67 stood between 8 and 10 points above the Finns and the A French Canadians. The Italians and the French Canadians taken as a group are on an entirely different level, 25 to 35 points below the central tendency for the American. The B French Canadians were lowest of all, scoring on an average but half the points scored by the American children. The central tendencies for the Beta scores show slighter differences. On the upper level the central tendencies for the Americans and Finns are both about 65 while the A group of French Canadians stands 5 or 6 points below. The gap between the upper and lower level is not so great as in the case of the Illinois scores, yet the two

general levels are still distinct. The Italians and French Canadians as a whole have central tendencies that lie 12 to 14 points below the Finns and Americans, while in the case of the B French Canadians it is 20 to 21.

6. The Americans are slightly above the norms for the Illinois test, while the Finns and A French Canadians are just at the average level of achievement for eleven year olds. The Italians are about two and the B French Canadians about three years below the normal mental age. In general the Beta scores correspond to the findings of Young.

7. Variability is about the same for all of the groups save the A and the B French Canadians. On the Illinois tests, in the case of the latter, a concentration of low scores, and in the case of the former, an absence of such scores explain the low variability. With the use of Beta the variability of the B French Canadians and the Italians increases tremendously relative to the variability of the Finns which seems to indicate a release from a handicap.

8. In the case of Illinois scores there is some overlapping, but while 15 per cent of the Finnish scores and 7 per cent of the A French Canadian scores lie above the American upper quartile none of the other groups have any significant number of scores reaching this point on the scale. The B French Canadian failed to even reach the American medican. Overlapping is greater in the case of Beta scores for 23 per cent of the Finns, 13 per cent of the A French Canadians and 12 per cent of the Italians exceed the upper quartile, although it is not quite attained by the B French Canadians.

9. The ranking of the various groups on the educational tests of reading and arithmetic corresponded to that on the intelligence tests but the French Canadians and Italians did better in arithmetic than in reading, while the reverse was true for the Americans. The performance of the Finns remained unchanged. Additional evidence from differential achievement quotients suggests the existence of a language handicap.

10. The occupation of the father and the number of rooms per person were taken as two indices of social status. According to both criteria the American children enjoyed the most favorable conditions. According to occupation of parent the French Cana-

dians came next followed by the Finns and finally the Italians. According to number of persons per room the Finns took second place while otherwise the order remained unchanged.

11. Correlations were worked out for the tests and other variables. Illinois and Beta scores gave a fairly high correlation with each other and with grade location. Illinois scores correlated higher with grade location than did the Beta. Some slight correlation of scores with social status was found. The Illinois test correlated higher than the Beta with both reading and arithmetic tests due to its verbal character and its weighting of the power factor in intelligence.

12. While there is danger of confusing deficiencies in the power aspect of intelligence with a linguistic handicap, yet the improved relative standing of certain groups with the use of a performance test, increased variability under these conditions, a differential performance on reading and arithmetic tests, coefficients of mean-square contingency indicating a relationship between the use of English in the home and test scores, and finally a differential achievement on sub-tests indicating difficulties for the foreign groups on verbal material, led to the conclusion that such a handicap exists.

13. A consideration of the discrepancy between the achievement of the A and B French Canadians was followed by the conclusion that actual differences in innate ability existed which were accentuated by the language handicap suffered by the B children.

14. The evidence points to the following general conclusions:

a. Americans are but slightly, if at all superior to the Finns in intelligence. Both are far above the Italians, and the French Canadians, taken as a whole, rank between these two extremes.

b. These differences are accentuated by a linguistic handicap.

c. The research confirms the evidence cited in Chapter II, indicating that marked differences in the intelligence of immigrant groups exist even when in the same environment, and the total evidence, with certain exceptions, is unfavorable to the "New Immigration," especially the Italians, so that the effect of immigration on American intelligence might be viewed with some concern.

d. The demonstration of a linguistic handicap means that these important differences in intelligence are less than they appear, but it fails to disprove their existence.

CHAPTER V

IMPLICATIONS OF THE FINDINGS AND SUGGESTIONS AS TO IMMIGRATION POLICY

The preceding chapters have stressed the importance of intelligence and have suggested the existence of considerable differences in the average intelligence of immigrant groups in this country. These differences even among children in the schools are really less than they appear to be, since test scores are often lowered by a linguistic handicap, but seem nevertheless very real differences. It remains to briefly point out the significance of these differences, to consider their implication regarding the effect of immigration on American intelligence and the value of past immigration policy, to discuss the recent immigration law and the principles on which it is based in the light of the findings, and finally, to make certain suggestions as to future policy.

SIGNIFICANCE OF GROUP DIFFERENCES

As will be pointed out, group differences are of much less importance than individual differences for a scientific attitude in connection with immigration or any other policy, demands that individuals be considered on their own merits rather than as members of a group, and yet they are very significant in several ways.

1. A knowledge of group differences indicates where talent or defect is likely to be found, thus aiding individual selection. An opportunity to select immigrants from a group of Englishmen making application for admission would probably be more profitable than an opportunity to select immigrants from an equal number of Italians, of the average type that have been coming to this country in such great numbers. On the other hand a social worker or other person interested in mental defect might be led to expect this condition to figure more prominently as a cause for maladjustment in one nationality as compared with another.

2. In the second place enough has been said and done to raise

105

the question of national and racial differences. Since prejudice will assert the worst, it is necessary to thrash out the matter until the truth is established, which in most cases will tend to be that the differences are not so extreme as bigots would claim, and that invariably a certain amount of overlapping exists. It is difficult to establish harmony and mutual appreciation even when no differences exist and still more so when exaggerated claims of superiority are based on a certain amount of truth. Since differences in ability associated with race or nationality make for prejudice and an approach to a caste system, the truth should be known and acted upon so as to obtain a homogeneity sufficient to make such an association of nationality with inferiority logically impossible (107).

3. Some of the most important implications of group differences are for educational policy taken in a broad sense. The success of programs of education and assimilation will depend in part upon a knowledge of the capacities and limitations of the people with which they deal. It is certain that differences in the average intelligence of various nationalities in this country can explain many puzzling differences in the success of schools of the same system but drawing from different elements in the population. There is still a tendency to place too much confidence in an assumed mental equality of individuals and groups. The best education will train to the limit of capacity but there is efficiency in the process in so far as sound knowledge and prevision replace a blundering trial and error process.

4. While individual selection is the ideal, group selection may be necessary as a temporary immigration policy, in fact we have it now under the recent immigration law, and the worth of such a policy can best be evaluated in the light of accurate knowledge of group differences.

5. Finally, the investigation of the general effect of recent immigration is a main purpose of the study and this can best be carried out by a comparison of various immigrant groups.

EVALUATION OF PAST IMMIGRATION POLICY

It is almost a mistake to speak of an immigration policy of the United States save in connection with recent times, and even then the demand for a supply of cheap labor to hasten the exploitation of the natural resources of the country was the dominating consideration. There was a supreme opportunity for developing a population of the highest quality in certain respects by the careful selection of immigrants, but that opportunity was little appreciated. In general the findings of this study are little to the credit of our immigration policy of the past. It should of course be remembered that the single trait of intelligence is not the only trait of social significance, nor do the innate traits dominate cultural considerations in importance. The Italians may have a musical ability that goes far to offset apparent deficiencies in other respects. Nevertheless, a careful consideration of the findings indicates that there is a serious tendency for groups, apparently of lower intelligence, to be the very groups that in the last two decades have come to this country in the greatest numbers. There are many exceptions. Some of the Jewish peoples seem possessed of considerable ability. The Finns, in Massachusetts at least, compare very favorably with the Americans. On the other hand the Italians, the Poles and the Russians probably have had a depressing effect on the average of American intelligence and the French Canadians certainly have not raised it. Since much of the evidence is derived from the achievement of school children rather than the immigrants themselves, even making due allowance for the influence of a language handicap, the findings are such as to raise grave doubts as to the success of the "Melting Pot." The differences between the immigrant stocks themselves are significant as suggesting that mental inferiority to American children is not merely environmental in origin. It is of course true that different people will draw different conclusions from the same facts, especially when varied and occasionally contradictory, but the writer is inclined to the view that probably the effect of immigration from 1900 on has been to lower the level of American intelligence. Further facts are greatly needed and upon them will depend the truth or falsity of this position.

The facts as to the amount of actual feeble-mindedness among the foreign-born are not so discouraging but nevertheless are far from satisfactory. While the army results that have been presented indicate that mental defect is only about one-half as frequent among the foreign- as compared with the native-born, yet that there are any at all shows that the immigration law forbidding the entrance of such persons has not worked perfectly. As Williams (138) has shown the difficulties of inspection are very great, yet while the numbers deported increased in the years following 1907 when the law was enacted, there is every reason to believe that large numbers of defectives still obtain entrance. Goddard (53) (54) found that after the government inspection feeble-minded individuals could be picked out by appearance from those that had passed the original inspection. The application of tests to these and others taken from those who had passed the regular examination revealed striking lack of intelligence. There has been some progress in the development and use of mental tests in connection with the arriving immigrant, but save for experimental studies (84) and the secondary examination, given when defect is suspected from appearance and response to questions, tests are not applied as a part of the procedure of inspection (131).

At the present time considerable numbers of feeble-minded are probably being admitted, for during the fiscal year ending June 30, 1923, the total number of immigrants certified as being feeble-minded, idiots or imbeciles, was but 107 (103, 142–143). Yet following a series of years in which the number of immigrants excluded for this cause was considerably greater, the examinations in the army disclosed considerable numbers of defectives among the foreign-born soldiers. The Italian defectives alone numbered 663 (7, 29) and if it is assumed that, as in the case of the population at large, 1.5 per cent of the men in the camps were of Italian birth, then out of 3,500,000 soldiers about 52,000 were Italians, of whom over 1 per cent were defective. It is of course possible that others were defective to slighter degree and were not detected.

DIFFERENTIAL BIRTH RATES

There is another aspect of the matter that makes the short comings of the past immigration policy more serious; namely, the matter of differential birth rates. Considerable evidence has been brought forth by Holmes (67, 125) Ross (108), Hill (66) and others to show the decline of the native stock, and while the famous Walker theory of immigration has been effectively criticized by Goldenweiser (56) and Davie (29) yet to a certain extent immigration must be regarded as a substitution of one stock for another (126). As Hewes (63) has shown the higher birth rate among immigrants does not disappear altogether with an improved standard of living. Much of the concern, however, that has arisen out of such facts is based on sentiment, for from the eugenic approach a differential birth rate is only significant when it is shown that the higher birth rate is associated with inferior qualities. The small amount of data collected in this study tends to suggest such an association. It was found that the average number of living children per family was 3.70 for the Americans, 3.56 for the Finns, 6.15 for the Italians, and 6.48 for the French Canadians. Since the child reporting in each case was eleven years of age, probably in most cases the families were nearly complete. The figures are of course large, compared with those that include sterile marriages, for there had to be at least one child to make the report. If the level of intelligence for the different groups remains as constant from generation to generation as does their stature, and we have some reason to think that this is the case, it will mean that the power for good or evil of certain immigrant groups is far greater than would be indicated by the numbers of the immigrants themselves. The Italian married adults of the present day are impressing their intelligence on the younger generation at a rate 50 or 60 per cent greater than the American married adults. Furthermore there is every probability that the Italian children studied will marry at an earlier age than the Americans. If differential death and marriage rates and marriage ages be disregarded, it is easy to see that of a hundred Americans and a hundred Italians in a few generations there would be several times as many Italians as Americans, if the relative size of family remained the same from generation to generation. After making all allowance for the imperfection of the methods of determining native intelligence and recognizing the probable decline in the birth rate of the native-born of foreign-born parents, still it is striking to find a high birth rate in the very groups that show low scores on intelligence tests.

Not only is there an inverse relationship between the intelligence of groups and the average number of children, but the same relationship tends to hold to a certain extent within the groups. Correlations were worked out for the various groups between the number of children in the family and the intelligence of the representative of the family tested in the school. In the case of the Americans there was a negative correlation of −0.038 P.E. 0.071, for the Finns it was −0.097 P.E. 0.059, for the Italians −0.044 P.E. 0.070, and for the French Canadians −0.262 P.E. 0.06. It is of course true that these correlations, while all negative are so small as to be insignificant in view of the size of the probable error. Yet the fact that they are consistently negative is suggestive. It is likely that if the data were more accurate the negative correlation would have increased. The work of Clark (23), who studied the size of family in relation to the intelligence of boys in the Whittier School, gave correlations of about the same size. In general the apparent tendency of the past immigration policy to lower the level of American intelligence is made more serious by the fact of a differential birth rate.

THE IMMIGRATION LAW OF 1924

The next task is a very brief discussion of the recent immigration law in the light of the findings. A number of improvements over previous legislation might be cited in favor of the law (100). It is based on an increased appreciation of biological factors, it decreases decidedly the numbers of immigrants, provision is made for the return of aliens after a temporary absence abroad, children take the nationality of their parents, the new arrangement as to monthly quotas will eliminate much inconvenience, and most important of all, there is provision for the issuance of visas by consular officers. This last is a step toward individual selection abroad. On the other hand the evidence that has been presented as to the mentality of the French Canadian and the Mexican is hardly such as to justify their classification as non-quota immigrants, at least on eugenic grounds.

In general the new immigration law is an attempt to shift the quotas in favor of the older immigration and in so doing it accords in a rough fashion with the findings that have been presented.

According to fairly reliable estimates (60, 10–11) the quota from Austria is reduced from 7451 to 1190, that of Greece from 3294 to 235, that of Hungary from 5638 to 688, that of Italy from 42,057 to 4089, that of Poland from 26,862 to 9072, and that of Russia from 21,613 to 1992, the proportionate deduction in these cases being considerably greater than that to which the north and west European countries were subjected. The standing of most of the countries whose quotas have been so sharply reduced tended to be low according to the various investigations previously cited.

Nevertheiess, while the law is roughly effective, it is most clumsy in its method of obtaining desired results, based as it is on the principle of group selection, by locality and race. The prevailing opinion supported in part by Laughlin's report before the Committee on Immigration, held that defect and inferiority were peculiar to immigrants of southern and eastern European birth, and this view with certain additional considerations as to assimilability operated powerfully to shift the percentage to 1890 as a base. We have seen that the Finns, at least in Massachusetts make a most creditable showing and yet the plan cuts down their quota from 3921 to but 345. Even according to Laughlin's data Ireland takes first place as a contributor to both insanity and dependency and to all defects taken together, while Austria-Hungary furnishes the lowest proportion of defective. Although Laughlin's data is open to question, still it is clear the sheep cannot be sharply separated from the goats on the basis of geography. Any scheme of group selection is bound to be inefficient when overlapping exists. There is not the slightest doubt that tremendous overlapping exists in the case of locality groups. The best of Southern Europeans are far superior to the poorest of the Northern Europeans. How foolish it would be for an employer to hire only men from a given section of the country even if on the average they tended to be slightly superior to the average of men from another section.

Another phase of group selection is that based on racial considerations, which represents a perversion of the proper stress on biological factors. Recently the Nordic myth has come into great prominence as a successor to the Aryan myth of Gobineau and Chamberlain and undoubtedly has had some influence in determining the immigration policy. According to the epic of Grant (59) and others, there arose in Europe a master race, tall of stature, blond of hair, blue of eye and long of head, whose members embodied most of the human virtues and were destined above other races to inherit the earth. After a glorious career as the bearers of the torch of civilization a Götterdammerung is imminent; the superior race tends to pass into extinction through bloody wars that inferior races are craven enough to avoid. Men like Grant (60), Gould (58), Burr (17), and Osborne (88) have their reactions to the immigration problem dominated to a great extent by ideas of racial superiority. The claims for Nordic superiority on the basis of cultural history and the Army tests have been effectively criticized by Boaz (11), Young (143), Smertenko (115), Bagley (6) and others, and must be regarded as resting on a very unsubstantial basis. There is no doubt that the physical differences between certain races may be accompanied by mental differences, but clear cut differences in mentality within the European stock seem very questionable. It should be stressed again at this point that none of the conclusions that have been drawn concerning the qualities of immigrant stocks can be considered as applying to nationalities as a whole, and even less to races. The possibilities of unfair selection are so great that it is impossible to reason from the part to the whole. Nothing more can be asserted than that there appear to be significant differences in the intelligence of certain of the immigrant groups in this country. A knowledge of these differences has a significance that has already been pointed out, but in view of the large amount of overlapping, individual selection is invariably more efficient than any group selection whether on the basis of locality, race or nationality.

A SUGGESTED IMMIGRATION POLICY

With due precaution against Utopian delusions, one may venture to set forth what seem to be the principles of a scientific immigration policy. 1, There should be individual selection based on scientific measurement and evaluation made as completely objective as possible. 2, Stress should be laid on what might be called the new mercantilism; a zeal for high grade immigrants, rather than a gold supply as in the 17th century, or in other words positive eugenics applied to immigration regulation. 3, There should be a minimum standard based on the average quality of the present population and a regulation of numbers by raising this standard. 4, Selection should be made on the other side. 5, There should be complete registration of the immigrants and an organization for their distribution and adjustment. 6, As suggested by Woolston (139, 670), it might be well to have a simple law administered by an executive commission aided by the advice of a research organization.

The idea of selective immigration is an old one and not altogether unfamiliar to statesmen as shown by the able plea for such a system made by Secretary Davis (30). The difficulties are considerable and of course that which is good and desirable and that which is likely to be acceptable are two different things. The effective operation of a selective plan designed to skim the cream from Europe depends on the development of objective tests of socially desirable traits. Much has been done along this line already for tests and examinations of all kinds have been developed and rating scales have come into use. Considerable progress has been made in the development of non-language tests[1] and there is no reason to think that it would be impossible to evolve a system of examination and rating that would in general select individuals of high capacity and general desirability (25) (118). A scale could be devised which would allow a certain number of points for various traits and qualifications. Mental capacity as determined by tests, education and training, freedom from taint of insanity, physical fitness, quality of parentage are among the considerations that should be taken into account. Final scores might consist of a weighted average of component scores for particular traits, or be the sum of the partial scores as in the case of a school examination where a certain amount of credit is given for each question. In any case a large amount of research and some arbitrary evaluation would be necessary in order to arrange a scale. If, for example, fitness is that of a Lionel Strongfort shall it receive the same number of points as the intelligence

[1] A committee of the National Research Council is engaged in the study of suitable tests for immigrants.

of a Steinmetz? Probably not, but the weighting of the various traits would have to be left to a research committee, and it is likely that a fairly satisfactory concensus of opinion could be obtained.

Turning to the second principle it must be pointed out that the whole tenor of immigration discussion is negative, centering around the means of preventing undesirable effects from immigration and it is now time for the positive side to be stressed. How shall we prevent undesirable immigration but also how shall we get desirable immigrants who will contribute more than they receive? It is after all a problem in positive eugenics for there is an excellent analogy between the breeding of a new generation of children and the bringing in of immigrants. Both affect the future character of society and both may be selected to a certain extent. It is true that the achievements of positive eugenics in determining which type of child shall be born are rather slight to date. There is far more surety in selecting an immigrant of known characteristics than an unborn child whose probable traits have their predictability limited by the present scant knowledge of the principles of heredity. It may be that a mercantilistic attitude even with respect to superior individuals savors of the nationalism that has cursed the world, but in another sense it is internationalistic in that it opens the road to talent wherever it may be. Bringing worthy representatives from one nation to another produces a cross-fertilization of culture, and by creating mutual respect, makes for international harmony and good will.

Given a method for estimating in exact terms the social desirability of a given individual what shall be the minimum requirements and how shall they be determined? One criterion is fairly obvious. No person should be admitted who does not measure up to the level of social desirability of the average American citizen, save as it may be necessary to make temporary exceptions for relatives of those already here. This would mean that every immigrant would be superior to about one-half of the present population. Such a minimum would tend to solve the problem of numbers as affecting assimilation and pressure on resources, but if necessary a limit might be established allowing the percentage of foreign-born to be only a fixed proportion of those here on a given date, say 1890. The numbers should be kept within the established limit by raising the minimum requirements thus making more rigid the selection. If more come over the wall than we can accommodate then we should raise the wall in order that those who do come shall be more strong and agile. The tremendous advantage of the selective plan described, aside from opening the road to talent and increasing our national vitality and cultural status, would be the avoidance of national or racial discrimination.

There are several objections that might be urged against a plan for selection in Europe. De Ward (34) is inclined to think that examination on foreign soil by officials would violate the sovereign rights of the nation concerned. It is true that if this new mercantilism ever came into vogue there would be no great enthusiasm for assisting another nation to draw away the best elements in the population. Still it is conceivable that unofficial examination might be arranged either by steamship companies or by mutual insurance companies. The latter would insure emigrants against financial loss by rejection and would be given preliminary examinations in order to prevent loss by rejections on this side. Of course such a plan would only be needed if the obstacles to official selection were insuperable. It remains to be seen how far the foreign governments will coöperate in furnishing data that the prospective immigrant may present to the Consul under the provisions of the present law.

The last two propositions of the list need little elaboration. There seems to be no way of stopping the growing practice of smuggling immigrants save by registration of immigrants until naturalized. Furthermore by registration it would be possible to check up as to the success with which legally admitted immigrants have become adjusted to their new environment. If a commission of ability could be obtained and entrusted with the duty of enforcing the spirit of a simple law it would probably make for efficiency.

It is Utopian to present an immigration policy in detail for there is little likelihood of a change in the near future. If it ultimately comes it will tend to be the resultant of a number of forces growing out of group interests rather than the rational outcome of a desire for the well being of society as a whole. Nevertheless there is a slowly growing respect for scientific investigation that may in the course of time give a certain influence to the considerable body of economists, psychologists and sociologists who are devoting themselves to the study of this vital problem.

BIBLIOGRAPHY

(1) ALEXANDER, H. B.: A comparison of the ranks of American States in Army Alpha and in social and economic status. Sch. and Soc., 1922, 16, pp. 388–92.

(2) Analysis of America's modern melting pot. Hearings before the Committee on Immigration and Naturalization. House of Rep. 67th Cong. 3rd Session Serial 7-C, pp. 725–831, Wash., 1923.

(3) ARLITT, A. H.: On the need for caution in establishing race norms. Jour. Applied Psych., 1921, 5, pp. 179–183.

(4) BABSON, H.: The Finns in Lanesville, Massachusetts. Studies in Sociology. Sociological Monograph No. 13, vol. iv, October, 1919, no. 1, Univ. of So. Cal.

(5) BAGLEY, W. C.: Do good schools pay? Jour. Nat. Ed. Ass., June 11, 1923, pp. 211–216.

(6) BAGLEY, W. C.: The Army Tests and the pro-Nordic propaganda. Ed. Review, April, 1924.

(7) BAILEY, P., AND HABER, R.: Mental deficiency. Reprint No. 94 from Mental Hygiene, vol. iv, no. 3, pp. 564–596, 1920.

(8) BELCOURT, N. A.: The French Canadians outside of Quebec. Ann. Amer. Acad., 107–108, p. 13 ff.

(9) BERRY, C. S.: The classification by tests of intelligence of ten thousand first grade pupils. Reprint from Jour. Educ. Research, October, 1922.

(10) BISHOP, O.: What is measured by the intelligence tests? Jour. Educ. Research, vol. ix, no. 1, January, 1924.

(11) BOAZ, F.: New York Times, April 13, 1924, ix, 19: 1.

(12) BORING, E. G.: The logic of the normal law of error in mental measurements. Amer. Jour. Psych., 1920, vol. 31, January, pp. 1–33.

(13) BORING, E. G.: Intelligence as the tests test it. New Rep., June 6, 1923, pp. 35–37.

(14) BRIDGES, J. W., AND COLER, L. E.: The relation of intelligence to social status. Psych. Rev., 1917, 24, 1–31.

(15) BRIGHAM, C. C.: A study of American intelligence. Princeton Press, 1923.

(16) BROWN, G. L.: Intelligence as related to nationality, Jour. Educ. Research, 1922, April, vol. 5, no. 4, pp. 324–327.

(17) BURR, C. S.: America's race heritage. The National Historical Society, 1922, N. Y.

(18) BURT, C.: Mental and scholastic tests. T. S. King, Lond., 1922.

(19) CATTELL, J. M.: American Men of Science, 3d ed., Science Press, 1921.

(20) CHAPMAN, J. C.: The unreliability of the difference between intelligence and educational ratings. Psych. Bull., vol. 20, no. 2, February, 1923, p. 89.

(21) CLEGHORN, K. H.: Methods of evaluating our immigrant peoples. Mental Hygiene, vol. vii, January, 1923, no. 1, p. 20 ff.

(22) CLARK, W. W.: Home Conditions and native intelligence. Jour. Delinq., 1922, 7: pp. 17–23.

(23) CLARK, W. W.: Birth rate and native intelligence. Psych. Clinic, 1922, 14, pp. 111–115.

(24) COLVIN, S. S., AND ALLEN, R. R.: Mental tests and linguistic ability, Jour. Educ. Psych., vol. xiv, January, 1923, no. 1, pp. 1 ff.

(25) CONKLIN, E. G.: Some biological aspects of immigration. Scrib. Mag., March, 1921, 69: pp. 352–359.

(26) COOLEY, C. H.: Genius, fame and the comparison of races, Ann. Amer. Acad., 9: pp. 317–358.

(27) DAVENPORT, C. B., AND CRAYTOR, L. C.: Comparative social traits of various races. Second study. Jour. Applied Psych., 1923, 7: 2: pp. 127 ff.

(28) DAVIDSON, P. E.: The social significance of the Army Intelligence findings. Sci. Mo., 1923, 16: pp. 184–195.

(29) DAVIE, M. R.: Immigration and the declining birthrate. Sci. Mo., 1924, 19: 1: July, pp. 68 ff.

(30) DAVIS, J. J.: Shall we restrict immigration? Forum, September, 1923, pp. 1857 ff.

(31) Decennial Census of Massachusetts for 1915. Wright and Potter, Boston, 1918.

(32) Decennial Census of Massachusetts, 1895, vol. ii.

(33) Decennial Census of Massachusetts, 1885, vol. i.

(34) DEC. WARD, R.: What next in immigration legislation? Sci. Mo., 1922, 15: 6: December, pp. 561–570.

(35) DEXTER, E. S.: The relation between occupation of parent and intelligence of children. Sch. & Soc., 1923, 17: pp. 612–614.

(36) DEXTER, R. C.: Fifty-fifty Americans. World's Work, August, 1924, pp. 366–71.

(37) DICKSON, V.: The intelligence of first grade children. Ph.D. Thesis, Stanford Univ. Library, 1919. Quoted by Young (151, 422).

(38) DUNLAP AND SNYDER: Jour. Exp. Psych., 1920, 3: pp. 396 ff.

(39) ELDERTON, E. M.: The relative strength of nature and nurture. Eugenic Laboratory Lecture Series, London.

(40) ELDERTON, E. M.: A summary of the present position with regard to the inheritance of intelligence. Biometrika, vol. 14, pp. 378 ff.

(41) FEINGOLD, G. A.: Intelligence of the first generation of immigrant groups. Jour. Educ. Psych., 1924, 15: 2: February, pp. 65 ff.

(42) FOERSTER, R. F.: The Italian Emigrant of Our Times. Harvard Univ. Press, Cambridge, 1919.

(43) FRYER, D.: Occupational intelligence standards. Sch. and Soc., 1922, 16: 272–7.

(44) FUKUDA, T.: Some data on the intelligence of Japanese children, Amer. Jour. Psych., 1923, 34: pp. 599–602.

(45) GALTON, F.: Inquiries into Human Faculty and Its Development. Dutton, N. Y.

(46) GALTON, F.: Hereditary Genius. Macmillan, Lond., 1892.

(47) GATES, A. I.: The unreliability of M.A. and I.O. based on group tests of general ability. Jour. Applied Psych., 1923, 7: pp. 93–100.

(48) GATES, A. I.: The correlations of achievement in school subjects with intelligence tests and other variables. Jour. Educ. Psych., March, 1922, 13: pp. 129 ff.

(49) GESELL, A.: Mental and physical correspondence in twins. Sci. Mo., April, 1922.

(50) GEYER, D. L.: Reliability of ratings by group intelligence tests. Jour. Educ. Psych., 1922, 13: pp. 43–9.

(51) GILLMAN, J. M.: Statistics and the immigration problem. Amer. Jour. Soc., July, 1924, 30: 1: 29 ff.

(52) GODDARD, H. H.: The Kallikak Family. Macmillan, N. Y., 1913.

(53) GODDARD, H. H.: Mental tests and the immigrant. Jour. Delinq., 2: 5: 243 ff.

(54) GODDARD, H. H.: The Binet tests in relation to immigration. Jour. Psycho-Asthenics, December, 1913, 18: 2: 105–107.

(55) GOLDENWEISER, A. A.: Race and culture in the modern world. Jour. Soc. Forces, November, 1924, 3: 1: 127 ff.

(56) GOLDENWEISER, E. A.: Walkers theory of immigration. Amer. Jour. Soc., 18: 342–51.

(57) GORDON, HUGH: Mental and scholastic tests of retarded children. Board of Educ. Pamphlet, No. 44, H. M. Stationery Office, Lond., 1923.

(58) GOULD, C. W.: America a Family Matter. Scribners, N. Y., 1922.

(59) GRANT, M.: The Passing of the Great Race. Scribners, N. Y., 1916–1919.

(60) GRANT, M.: The racial transformation of America. No. Am. Rev., March, 1924, 219: 3: 342 ff.

(61) GRIER, N. M.: Comparative mentality of Jews and Gentiles. Ped. Sem., December, 1918, 25: 432–433.

(62) GUIFFRIDA-RUGGERI: The origins of the Italian people. Amer. Jour. Phys. Anth., 1918, 1: 318 ff.

(63) HEWES, AMY: Note on the racial and educational factors in the declining birth-rate. Amer. Jour. Soc., September, 1923, 29: 2: 17 ff.

(64) HEXTER, M., AND MYERSON, A.: 13.77 versus 12.05; A study in probable error. Mental Hygiene, January, 1924, 8: 1.

(65) HILDON, KAARLO: Die Anthropologische Erforschung Finnlands. Archiv. f. Anthrop., 19: 36–40. Heft. 1, 1922.

(66) HILL, J. A.: Comparative fecundity of native and foreign parentage. Qu. Pub. Am. Stat. Ass., 13: 583–604.

(67) HOLMES, S. J.: The Trend of the Race. Harcourt Brace, N. Y., 1921.

(68) The Interpreter, 1924, 3: 5.
(69) JACKSON, G. E.: Emigration of Canadians to the United States. Ann. Am. Acad., 1923, 107–108: 25 ff.
(70) JENKS, J. W., AND LAUCK, W. J.: The Immigration Problem. Fifth ed., Funk and Wagnalls, N. Y., 1922.
(71) JENNINGS, H. S.: Heredity and environment. Sci. Mo., 1924, 19: 3: 225 ff.
(72) JORDAN, A. M.: Correlations of four intelligence tests with grades. Jour. Educ. Psych., 1922, 13: 7: 419 ff.
(73) JORDAN, R. H.: Nationality and school progress. Public School Pub. Co., Bloomington, Ill., 1921.
(74) KELLEY, T. L.: Statistical Method. Macmillan, N. Y., 1923.
(75) KELLEY, T. L.: The measurement of overlapping. Jour. Educ. Psych., 1919, 10: 458 ff.
(76) LEAMING, R. E.: A study of a small group of Irish-American children. Psych. Clinic, 1923, 15: 18–40.
(77) LODGE, H. C.: Distribution of ability in the United States. Cent. Mag., September, 1891.
(78) MADSEN, I. N.: Some results with the Stanford Revision of the Binet-Simon Tests. Sch. and Soc., May 10, 1924, 19: 489: 556–562.
(79) MARQUIS, G. E.: The French Canadians in the Province of Quebec. Ann. Am. Acad., 1923, 107–108: 7.
(80) McFADDEN, J. H., AND DASHIELL, J. F.: Racial differences as measured by the Downey Will-Temperament Test. Jour. Applied Psych., 1923, 7: 1: 30 ff.
(81) Memoirs of the National Academy of Sciences, vol. xv, 1921.
(82) MERRIMAN, C.: The intellectual resemblance of twins. Psych. Mon., 1924, 33: 5 (Whole No. 152).
(83) MONROE, W. S.: The Illinois Examination. Bureau of Educ. Research. Bull. No. 6. University of Illinois Bulletin, 1921, 19: 9.
(84) MULLEN, E. H.: Mentality of the arriving emigrant. U. S. P. H. S. Bull. 90, Govt. Prt. Off., Wash., 1917.
(85) MURDOCK, K.: Race differences in New York City. Sch. and Soc., 1920, 11: 147–150.
(86) MURDOCK, K.: A study of mental differences which are due to race. Psych. Bull., 1924, 21: 2: 108.
(87) OGBURN, W. F.: Social Change. Huebsch, N. Y., 1922.
(88) OSBORNE, H. F.: New York Times, April 8, 1924, 18: 7.
(89) PARMELEE, M.: The Science of Human Behavior. Macmillan, N. Y., 1913.
(90) PASCHAL, F., AND SULLIVAN, L. R.: An anthropological and psychological analysis of Mexican school children in Tucson, Arizona. Psych. Bull., February, 1924, 109 ff.
(91) PEAKE, H.: Some notes on the Finnic problem. Rep. Brit. Ass. Adv. Sci., 1919, 282 ff.

(92) PEARSON, K.: The scope and importance to the state of the science of national eugenics. Eug. Lab. Lect., Series No. 1, Lond.

(93) PINTNER, R.: A comparison of the ranks of American States in Army Alpha and in social and economic status. Sch. and Soc., 1922, 16: 388–92.

(94) PINTNER, R., AND KELLER, R.: Intelligence tests of foreign children. Jour. Educ. Psych., 1922, 13: 214 ff.

(95) PINTNER, R.: Comparison of American and foreign children on intelligence tests. Jour. Educ. Psych., 1923, 14: 292–295.

(96) PINTNER, R.: Intelligence Testing Methods and Results. Holt, N. Y., 1923.

(97) POPENOE, P., AND JOHNSON, R.: Applied Eugenics. Macmillan, N. Y., 1923.

(98) PORTEUS, S. D.: Temperament and mentality in maturity, sex and race. Jour. Applied Psych., March, 1924, 8: 1: 57 ff.

(99) PRESSEY, S. S., AND RALSTON, R.: The relation of the general intelligence of school children to the occupation of their fathers. Jour. Applied Psych., 1919, 3: 366–373.

(100) Public —— No. 139 68th Cong. H. R. 7995. Govt. Prt. Off.

(101) PYLE, W. H.: A study of the mental and physical characteristics of the Chinese. Sch. and Soc., August 31, 8, 192: 264–269.

(102) READE, A.: Finland and the Finns. Dodd, N. Y., 1917.

(103) Report of the Commissioner General of Immigration, 1923. Wash. Govt. Prt. Off., 1923.

(104) Reports of the Immigration Commission. The children of immigrants in schools (in 5 vols). Vol. I, 61st. Cong. 3d Sess. Doc. 749. Wash. Govt. Prt. Off., 1911.

(105) RIPLEY, W. Z.: The Races of Europe. Appleton, N. Y., 1899.

(106) ROOT, W. I.: Correlation of group tests. Jour. Educ. Psych., 1922, 13: 286 ff.

(107) ROSS, E. A.: The menace of migrating peoples. Cent. Mag., May, 1921, 131–5.

(108) ROSS, E. A., AND BABER, R. E.: Slow suicide among our native stock. Cent. Mag., February, 1924, 504 ff.

(109) RUCH, G. M., AND KOERTH, W.: "Power" vs. "Speed" in Army Alpha. Jour. Educ. Psych., April, 1923, 14: 4: 193 ff.

(110) RUCH, G. M.: The speed factor in mental measurements. Jour. Educ. Research, 1924, 9: 1: 39 ff.

(111) RUGG, H. O.: Statistical Methods Applied to Education. Houghton Mifflin, N. Y., 1917.

(112) SAER, D. J.: The effect of bilingualism on intelligence. Brit. Jour. Psych., 1923, 14: 25–38.

(113) SAER, D. J.: An inquiry into the effect of bilingualism upon the intelligence of young children. Jour. Exp. Pedagogy, 1922, 6: 266 ff.

(114) SHELDON, W. H.: The intelligence of Mexican children. Sch. and Soc., February, 1924, 19: 139–142.

(115) Smertenko, J. J.: The claim of "Nordic" race superiority. Curr. Hist., April, 1924, pp. 15 ff.

(116) Smith, F.: Bilingualism and mental development. Brit. Jour. Psych., 1923, 13: 271–282.

(117) Starch, D.: Educational Psychology. Macmillan, N. Y., 1920.

(118) Sweeney, A.: Mental tests for immigrants. No. Am. Rev., 1922, 215: 600–612.

(119) Swift, E. D.: Some strange memories. Scrib. Mag., September, 1923.

(120) Symonds, P. M.: The intelligence of Chinese in Hawaii. Sch. and Soc., 1924, 19: 486: 442 ff.

(121) Symposium: Intelligence and its measurement. Jour. Educ. Psych., 1921, 12: 123–147; 195–216.

(122) Tables to facilitate the computation of coefficients of correlation by the rank difference method. Scott Company Lab. Jour Applied Psych., 1920, 4: 115–125.

(123) Taussig, F. L.: Principles of Economics, Vol. II. Macmillan, N. Y., 1911.

(124) Terman, L. M.: The psychological determinist or democracy and the I.Q. Jour. Educ. Research, Reprint, June, 1922.

(125) Thompson, M.: Validity of Stanford-Binet Tests as a basis of prediction of school success. M.A. Thesis, Stanford Univ., 1920.

(126) Thompson, W. S.: Standards of living as they affect the growth of competing population groups. Sci. Mo., July, 1923, 17: 1: 57 ff.

(127) Thorndike, E. L.: Measurements of twins. Archives of Phil. Psych. and Sci. Methods, no. 1.

(128) Thorndike, E. L.: Tests of intelligence, reliability, significance, susceptibility to special training and adaptation to general nature of the task. Sch. and Soc., 1919, 9: 189–195.

(129) Torps, H. A., and Symonds, P. M.: What shall we expect of the A.Q.? Jour. Educ. Psych., 1922, 13: 513–528 and 1923, 14: 27–28.

(130) Twenty-First Year Book of the National Soc. for the Study of Educ. Public School Pub. Co. Bloomington, Ill., 1922.

(131) U. S. P. H. S. Manual of the Mental Examination of Aliens. Misc. Pub. 18. Wash. Govt. Prt. Off., 1918.

(132) Van Cleef, E.: The Finn in America. Geog. Rev., 6: 3: 184–214.

(133) Walcott, G. D.: The intelligence of Chinese students. Sch. and Soc., 1920, 11: 474–480.

(134) Ward, L. F.: Eugenics, euthenics, eudemics. Am. Jour. Soc., 1913, 18: 6, 737.

(135) Ward, L. F.: Applied Sociology. Ginn, Boston, 1916.

(136) Woods, F. A.: Heredity and the hall of fame. Pop. Sci. Mo., May, 1913.

(137) Woods, F. A.: Mental and moral heredity in royalty. Holt, N. Y.. 1906.

(138) WILLIAMS, L. L.: The medical examination of mentally defective aliens; its scope and limitations. Am. Jour. Insanity, 1914, 71: 2: 257–268.

(139) WOOLSTON, H.: Wanted—an American immigration policy. Jour. Soc. Forces, September, 1924, 2: 5: 666–670.

(140) YEUNG, K. T.: The intelligence of Chinese children in San Francisco and vicinity. Jour. Applied Psych., 1921, 5: 267–274.

(141) YOAKUM, C. S., AND YERKES, R. M.: Army Mental Tests. Holt, N. Y., 1920.

(142) YOUNG, K.: The history of mental testing. Ped. Sem., 1924, 31: 1: 1–48.

(143) YOUNG, K.: Review of "American intelligence." Science, 57: 1484: 666–670.

(144) YOUNG, K.: Intelligence tests of certain immigrant groups. Sci. Mo., 1922, 15: 417–434.

(145) YOUNG, K.: Mental differences in certain immigrant groups. Univ. of Oreg. Pub., 1922, 1: 11:

(146) YULE, G. U.: Introduction to the Theory of Statistics. 5th ed. Griffin, Lond., 1919.

INDEX

Americans, intelligence of, 24, 25, 26, 28, 30, 31, 32, 34, 35, 38, 40, 50, 60, 62, 63–65; birth rate of, 109

Arlitt, on social status and test scores, 35, 81

Army tests, 15–17; correlation of scores with mental defect, 23; comparison with results of, 26

Assimilation, 2

Austrians, intelligence of, 16, 17, 24, 38, 43, 45, 49, 50

Bagley, 18, 21, 22, 112
Bailey and Haber, 22, 47
Belcourt, 54
Belgians, intelligence of, 16, 17, 43
Berry, report on mental testing, 27–28
Beta, 16, 19; test, description of, 57; sub-tests, analysis of, 95–97
Bishop, on practice effects, 21
Bohemians, intelligence of, 36, 40, 50
Boaz, 112
Boring, 6, 9, 18
Bridges, findings regarding intelligence and social status, 81
Brigham, 16, 17, 19, 20, 23
Brown, research results, 24
Burr, 112
Bust, 22

Canadians, intelligence of, 16, 17, 28, 40, 43, 49, 50
Central tendencies, comparison of, 67–68
Cleghorn, 15
Cleveland clinical data, 36
Correlations, 9, 10, 23, 33, 41, 83–86; by coefficient of mean-square-contingency, 88; of intelligence and size of family, 110
Culture, nature of culture change, 3

Danes, intelligence of, 16, 17, 26, 38, 43, 50
Davidson, 20
Davie, 109
Davis, 113
De Ward, 115
Degeneracy, 3, 11
Democracy, Intelligence and, 4
Dexter, E. S., 85
Dexter, R. C., 54
Dickson, 31
Differential Birth Rates, 108–110
Dunlap and Snyder, on practice effects, 20
Dutch, intelligence of, 16, 17, 43, 49, 50

Economic, aspects of immigration, 1–2, 36, 55
Education, intelligence necessary for, 4; and test scores, 21–24, 31–32
Educational Achievement Tests, results of, 77–80
Eminence, resemblances in, 10; and nationality, 42–44; see various nationality groups, intelligence of
English, intelligence of, 16, 17, 24, 26, 28, 34, 38, 40, 43, 45, 49, 50
Environment, test scores and, 19–24; and retardation, 41–42

Feingold, research of, 25–27
Finns, intelligence of, 24, 34, 38, 50, 60, 61, 62, 63–65; sociological background of, 55; birth rate of, 109
Fitchburg, 54
Foreign-speaking children, see linguistic handicap
French, intelligence of, 24, 26, 43, 49, 50
French Canadians, intelligence of, 40, 50, 62, 63–65; anthrópological

125